EXPERIENCE

MALTA

IN 2024 & BEYOND

A Practical Pocket Guide For All Travelers

Sammy J. Jones

Copyright © by Sammy J. Jones 2024.

All rights reserved.

Except for brief quotations used in critical reviews and other non-commercial uses permitted by copyright law, no part of this publication may be copied, distributed, or transmitted in any way without the publisher's prior written consent, including by photocopying, recording, or other electronic or mechanical methods.

The use of any trademarks or brands mentioned in this book is solely for the purpose of clarification and is not intended to imply any affiliation with the respective owners of those marks or brands.

Map of Malta

[Click here to View the Map of Malta](#) (For e-book readers)

Scan the QR Code below with your mobile phone's Camera to View the Map of Malta (For Paperback Readers).

3

TABLE OF CONTENTS

Map of Malta

INTRODUCTION

    Discovering Malta's Rich History

CHAPTER 1

Practical Tips for Travelers

    Visa Requirements and Entry Guidelines

    Health and Safety Information

    Packing Essentials for Malta

    Money and Expenses

    Best Times to Visit

    Cultural Etiquette and Local Customs

    Language Basics

CHAPTER 2

Getting There and Around

    How to Get There: Air and Sea Travel

    Getting Around: Transportation Tips

CHAPTER 3

Accommodation Options

    Hotels: From Luxury to Budget

    Boutique Hotels and Historic Inns

    Family-Friendly Stays and Resorts

    Unique Accommodations: Farmhouses and Heritage Homes

Booking Tips and Recommended Platforms
CHAPTER 4
Culinary and Dining Experience
  Local Cuisine and Must-Try Dishes
  Top Restaurants Across Malta
  Cooking Classes and Culinary Tours
CHAPTER 5
Shopping and Souvenirs
  Markets and Street Vendors
  Boutique Shopping in Valletta and Mdina
  Souvenir Shopping: Local Handicrafts and Unique Finds
CHAPTER 6
Top Attractions and Activities
  History and Culture of Valletta
  Must-Visit Sites: St. John's Co-Cathedral, Lascaris War Rooms, Upper & Lower Barrakka Gardens
  Museums: National War Museum, National Archaeology Museum, Malta at War Museum
  Gozo: The Island Sanctuary
  Historical Sites: Ggantija Temples, The Old Prison
  Natural Beauty: Ta' Cenc Cliffs, Ninu's Cave
  Cultural Museums: Gozo Archaeology

Museum, Gozo Cathedral Museum

CHAPTER 7

Hidden Gems

    Walking Through History: Streets of Mdina and Rabat

    Cultural Sites: St. Paul's Catacombs, Roman Villa, Natural History Museum

    Exploring the Blue Lagoon

    Comino's Hiking Trails and Viewpoints

    Wildlife and Nature Reserves

CHAPTER 8

Southern Malta: The Archaeological Region

    Hagar Qim & Mnajdra Temples

    Exploring the Blue Grotto

    Coastal Walks at Mtahleb Cliffs

CHAPTER 9

Northern Malta: Coastal Adventures

    Mellieha: Popeye Village and Beaches

    St. Paul's Bay: National Aquarium and Coastal Charm

    Birdwatching and Nature Trails at Salina National Park

CHAPTER 10

Central Malta : Activities

    Aviation Museum

Mosta Dome: Marvel at One of the World's Largest Church Domes
Qormi: Bread-Making and Local Festivities
CHAPTER 11
Western Malta: Landscapes and History
Mtarfa: Military History and Natural Sights
Dingli Cliffs: Sunset Views and Nature Walks
Exploring San Anton Gardens
CHAPTER 12
Entertainment and Nightlife
Paceville: The Heart of Nightlife
Nightlife and Entertainment: Bars, Clubs, and Live Music
Casino and Entertainment Options
Mediterraneo Marine Park and Splash & Fun Water Park
Festivals and Events: A Year-Round Guide
CHAPTER 13
Exploring Malta by Traveler Type
Solo Travelers: Tips and Safe Practices
Couples: Romantic Spots and Activities
Family Adventures: Kid-Friendly Attractions and Dining
Senior Travelers: Accessibility and Leisure Options

CHAPTER 14
Day Trips and Extended Excursions
- Planning Day Trips from Major Cities
- Guided Tours vs. Self-Guided Explorations

CHAPTER 15
Itineraries
- Quick Getaways: 3-Day Itineraries
- Weeklong Explorations: Comprehensive 7-Day Tours
- Specialized Itineraries: Adventure, Culture, and Relaxation

CHAPTER 16
Essential Information and Services
- Travel Scams and How to Avoid Them
- Emergency Services and Contacts
- Communication: SIM Cards and Internet Access
- LGBTQ+ Travel Considerations
- Road Trip Routes and Scenic Drives
- Free Tourist Attractions
- Paid Tourist Attractions
- Useful Apps and Websites

CONCLUSION

INTRODUCTION

Malta, an archipelago in the center of the Mediterranean, blends centuries of history with a vibrant cultural scene and stunning natural beauty. This guide unlocks the treasures of Malta, offering insights and information that turn a simple visit into an extraordinary adventure. Whether traveling alone, with a loved one, or with family, Malta presents a diverse tapestry of experiences to suit all interests.

The heart of Malta's charm lies in its rich history, visible in the architecture and ancient sites spread across the island. From the bustling streets of Valletta, the capital city known for its strategic importance and architectural marvels, to the silent, timeless streets of Mdina, the old capital, Malta tells the story of a past marked by knights, battles, and legacy.

In Valletta, we dive into a world where history is displayed in every corner, from the majestic fortifications to the ancient edifices that line its streets. Walking through Valletta is like stepping back in time, with each building and alley holding its own story. Here, we explore hidden gems and learn about the knights who once made this city their home.

Moving away from the cities, Malta's landscape offers equally compelling attractions. The cliffs of Dingli offer sweeping views of the sea, while the Blue Lagoon on Comino Island is a slice of paradise with its crystal-clear waters and tranquil vibes. Our guide provides tips on the best times to visit these natural wonders to avoid the crowds and fully enjoy the serene beauty.

Maltese cuisine is a highlight not to be missed. Influenced by Italian, Middle Eastern, and local flavors, Maltese food is a delight to explore. This guide takes you beyond the typical tourist spots to where the locals eat and enjoy. Discover the best places for traditional pastizzi, fresh seafood, and the unique flavors of Maltese wines.

Beyond the sights and flavors, this guide equips you with all the practical knowledge needed for a seamless travel experience. From navigating the local transportation system to choosing accommodations that fit your needs and budget, we cover all the essentials. Detailed maps, travel tips, and customized itineraries help you plan your stay, whether it's for a few days or a longer exploration.

This guide doesn't just list destinations; it enhances your understanding of Malta and enriches your experience. Every chapter is designed to bring you closer to the authentic heart of Malta, making your visit not just a trip, but a journey of discovery. So, get ready to explore the islands and create unforgettable memories in this unique Mediterranean gem.

Discovering Malta's Rich History

Malta's history is as rich and diverse as the Mediterranean itself, with layers of civilization built one atop the other, each leaving a mark that can still be seen and felt today. This small island nation has been a strategic prize for conquerors and a haven for traders throughout the centuries. From ancient temples to the silent fortifications of wartime, Malta offers a timeline that stretches back thousands of years.

The earliest signs of human activity in Malta date back to around 5900 BCE. These first inhabitants likely came from Sicily, about 100 kilometers to the north. They built some of the world's oldest free-standing structures, the Megalithic Temples, which predate even the pyramids of Egypt. These temples, such as Ħaġar Qim, Mnajdra, and the Ggantija, are among the most sophisticated architectural feats of their time, featuring intricate stonework without the use of metal tools, wheels, or mortar. By about 1000 BCE, the Phoenicians, skilled sailors and traders from what is now Lebanon, discovered the islands. They used Malta as an outpost to expand their trading networks across the Mediterranean. The Phoenicians were followed by the Romans in 218 BCE, who gave Malta its first roads, coins, and extensive urban development, evidence of which can still be seen in the ruins scattered across the island, particularly in Rabat and Mdina.

The middle ages brought a series of rulers to Malta, from the Byzantines to the Arabs, and finally the Normans. Each group left its linguistic and cultural imprint on the island. The Arabic influence remains strong in the Maltese language, which contains many Arabic words and roots. The Normans and subsequent rulers reinforced Christianity in Malta, which is evident in the abundance of churches and religious festivals that play a central role in Maltese culture today. One of the most defining periods in Maltese history began in 1530 when the islands were handed over to the Knights of St. John. The Knights, a military and charitable order, made Malta their base after being expelled from Rhodes by the Ottoman Turks. They transformed Valletta, the capital city, into a fortified urban center. The Great Siege of 1565, a pivotal battle in which the Knights, aided by the local Maltese, successfully held off the invading Ottoman Turks, is one of the most celebrated events in Malta's history. The victory not only secured Malta's place as a stronghold but also enhanced its architectural and artistic heritage, much of which was commissioned by the Knights as a form of thanks and celebration.

British rule in the 19th and early 20th centuries introduced new architectural styles and infrastructures, including schools, hospitals, and the Royal Opera House. Malta's strategic position once again made it a focal point during World War II, enduring extensive bombings and a blockade that tested the resilience of its people. In 1964,

Malta achieved independence, and in 1974 it became a republic.

Today, Malta is a blend of cultures that reflects its complex past. The island is proud of its heritage and preserves its history with care and respect. Visitors can see this history in the preserved architecture, museums, and ancient sites. The story of Malta is a narrative of resilience and adaptation, visible in every stone and artifact that dots the island.

Exploring Malta's history is not just about visiting museums or sites. It's about understanding the layers of human endeavor and the spirit of a people shaped by their geography and the successive waves of influences brought by settlers, conquerors, and visitors through the ages. This narrative enriches the experience of every traveler who steps onto the island, offering not just a holiday destination but a journey through time.

CHAPTER 1

Practical Tips for Travelers

Embarking on a trip to Malta promises a wealth of experiences, from its sun-drenched coastlines to its history-steeped streets. To help you make the most of your visit, this chapter provides essential tips tailored for travelers. We'll cover practical aspects that include how to navigate visa requirements and what you should know about entering Malta, ensuring you start your journey smoothly.

We also discuss important health and safety tips to keep you protected while exploring. Whether it's knowing the nearest health facilities or understanding local hazards, we have you covered. Additionally, this chapter includes invaluable advice on what to pack to suit Malta's climate and social settings, so you can blend in comfortably and enjoy your activities without hassle. Managing your finances is another crucial aspect we'll explore. Understanding the local currency, average costs, and budgeting tips will help you manage your expenses effectively. We'll guide you through everything from dining costs to souvenir shopping, so you can make informed spending choices.

Furthermore, learning about the best times to visit can enhance your travel plans, allowing you to choose a period that matches your preferences for weather and local events. Insights into cultural etiquette and local customs will also prepare you for interactions with Maltese residents, enriching your travel experience by fostering respect and understanding.

Lastly, we'll touch on language basics. While English is widely spoken, learning a few phrases in Maltese can go a long way in showing respect and enhancing your communication with locals.

This chapter is designed to equip you with all the practical knowledge needed for a fulfilling trip to Malta, allowing you to navigate the island with confidence and ease.

Visa Requirements and Entry Guidelines

Understanding the visa requirements and entry guidelines for Malta is essential for any traveler planning a visit. This section aims to provide you with a clear and straightforward overview of what you need to prepare before you travel, ensuring a smooth entry process when you arrive.

Malta is a member of the European Union and part of the Schengen Area, which means that the visa requirements for Malta are in line with those of other Schengen countries. If you are a citizen of another EU country, you can enter Malta using just your national ID card or passport, with no need for a visa. You have the right to stay for an unlimited period, but you must register with local authorities if you plan to live there for more than three months. For non-EU citizens, the requirements vary depending on your nationality. Many countries, including the United States, Canada, Australia, and New Zealand, are part of the visa-exemption program. This allows their citizens to enter Malta without a visa for stays of up to 90 days within a 180-day period. During this time, you can travel freely within the Schengen Zone, but you cannot engage in paid work.

If you come from a country that is not visa-exempt, you will need to apply for a Schengen visa. This visa is also valid for up to 90 days within a six-month period and is applicable for tourism, visiting family or friends, or business.

To apply for a visa, you need to provide several documents, including a passport that is valid for at least three months beyond your planned departure from the Schengen area, travel medical insurance coverage of at least 30,000 euros, proof of accommodation, and evidence that you have sufficient funds for your stay. You may also need to provide a travel itinerary and a letter explaining the purpose of your visit. It's important to apply for your visa well in advance of your trip, ideally at least 15 days before you intend to travel, but you can apply up to six months in advance. Visa applications are submitted through the consulate or embassy of Malta in your home country, or a visa application center if there is no Maltese diplomatic mission.

Upon arrival in Malta, all travelers must present their valid travel documents. Additionally, border control may ask you questions about your trip, such as the duration of your stay and the purpose of your visit, to ensure that you meet the entry conditions. They might also ask to see your return ticket and proof of sufficient funds for the duration of your stay.

Understanding and preparing for Malta's visa and entry requirements is crucial for a hassle-free visit. By ensuring that you have all the necessary documents and information, you can look forward to enjoying all that Malta has to offer without any complications at the border.

Health and Safety Information

Traveling to Malta offers a chance to experience its beautiful landscapes, historical sites, and vibrant culture. However, staying healthy and safe is crucial to ensure a pleasant trip. This section covers important health and safety information for visitors to Malta.

Firstly, Malta's healthcare system is well-regarded, with both public and private hospitals that provide good medical services. In case of a medical emergency, dialing 112 will connect you to emergency services. For minor health issues, pharmacies are widely available, and pharmacists can offer advice and over-the-counter medications. It's advisable to carry a European Health Insurance Card (EHIC) if you are from an EU country, as this will cover you for most medical services in public healthcare facilities at a reduced cost or for free. Travelers from outside the EU should have comprehensive travel health insurance. Regarding health precautions, Malta has a warm climate, and sun exposure can be significant, especially in summer. To avoid sunburn, dehydration, or heatstroke, wear sunscreen, stay hydrated, and seek shade during the hottest part of the day, typically from 11 a.m. to 3 p.m. Despite the heat, Malta's tap water is safe to drink, but some visitors prefer bottled water due to the taste of local tap water. Safety in Malta is generally not a big concern as it is one of the safer countries in Europe. Violent crime rates are low, but as in any tourist destination, you should be cautious of pickpocketing and petty theft, especially in crowded areas. Always keep an eye on your belongings, and use safes for valuables in hotels.

Malta has a good network of roads, but driving can be challenging due to narrow streets and sometimes aggressive driving styles. If you choose to rent a car, make sure you are comfortable with left-hand driving, as it follows the British system. Also, familiarize yourself with local traffic laws to avoid fines. For those who prefer not to drive, Malta has an extensive public bus system that reaches most parts of the island. Taxis and ride-sharing services are also available and are a safe and reliable way to travel around.

For those who enjoy swimming, Malta offers many beautiful beaches. However, always pay attention to flag warnings at beaches and follow local advice about swimming conditions. Some areas may have strong currents or jellyfish that could pose risks.

Staying informed about health and safety practices in Malta will help ensure that your visit is enjoyable and worry-free. Preparing for the climate, understanding healthcare options, staying vigilant about personal safety, and knowing how to move around safely are all parts of making your trip successful. By taking these simple precautions, you can focus on enjoying the rich experiences that Malta has to offer.

Packing Essentials for Malta

Packing for a trip to Malta requires thoughtful preparation to ensure you have everything needed for a comfortable and enjoyable visit. Malta's Mediterranean climate, range of activities, and cultural norms dictate a specific packing list that balances practicality with respect for local customs. Start with the basics: clothing. Malta enjoys warm, sunny weather for the majority of the year, with hot summers and mild winters. Lightweight and breathable clothing are essential for the summer months. Include items such as T-shirts, shorts, and light dresses. A hat and sunglasses are crucial to protect against the sun. Despite the heat, it's wise to pack a light jacket or sweater for cooler evenings and air-conditioned venues.

Footwear should be comfortable and versatile. Expect to do a lot of walking, often on uneven surfaces, especially in historic areas like Valletta or Mdina. Durable walking shoes are a must. If you plan to visit beaches or enjoy water activities, bring along a pair of water shoes to protect against rocky surfaces and hot sand. Malta is a popular destination for swimming and sunbathing, so don't forget to pack your swimwear. A beach towel and a reusable water bottle are also handy, helping you stay hydrated and comfortable during beach days or long walks. Sunscreen is another critical item, as the Maltese sun can be quite strong, especially between June and August.

Regarding technology, ensure you have an adapter for Malta's power sockets, which are typically the three-pin type G, the same as in the United Kingdom. A power bank is useful for long days out when you might not have access to a charging point. If you are planning to capture the beauty of Malta, whether its urban scenery or coastal views, remember to pack your camera or ensure your phone has enough space and capability for photos and videos. For personal health, pack a basic first-aid kit that includes medication for common ailments like headaches or stomach upset, as well as plasters and antiseptic cream for minor cuts or scrapes. If you have prescription medication, bring enough for the duration of your stay, along with a copy of your prescription in case you need to explain it at customs or refill it locally.

Malta is a predominantly Catholic country, and visiting churches is a popular activity. When packing, include some modest clothing that covers shoulders and knees to respect local customs, especially in religious sites. Finally, if you're visiting during the winter months, from December to February, the weather can be cooler and occasionally rainy. A waterproof jacket and a pair of sturdy, water-resistant shoes will make your stay more comfortable. By packing thoughtfully for Malta, considering the weather, activities, and cultural aspects, you ensure a smooth and respectful experience exploring all that this beautiful island nation has to offer.

Money and Expenses

Understanding money and expenses is crucial for anyone planning to visit Malta. This guide provides an overview of the currency, typical costs, and tips on managing your budget while enjoying everything Malta has to offer.

Malta uses the Euro (€) as its official currency, making it convenient for travelers from other Eurozone countries who don't need to worry about exchanging money. For visitors from outside the Eurozone, it's recommended to exchange some currency before arriving or withdraw Euros from ATMs located throughout the islands.

When it comes to managing daily expenses, Malta offers options for various budgets. Eating out, for instance, can vary significantly in cost. Local eateries and smaller towns often provide meals at lower prices than the more tourist-centric areas. A typical meal at an inexpensive restaurant might cost between €10 to €15, while dining at a mid-range restaurant can set you back about €25 to €40 per person, including drinks.

Accommodation costs in Malta also vary. Budget travelers can find hostels and budget hotels ranging from €15 to €50 per night. Mid-range hotels typically charge between €60 and €120 per night, whereas luxury accommodations can cost significantly more, especially during peak tourist season from June to September.

Public transportation in Malta is efficient and affordable. Buses are the main mode of transport and cover extensive routes across all major towns and attractions. A single journey ticket costs around €2, but for longer stays, consider purchasing a multi-day pass that offers unlimited travel and can significantly reduce your transportation costs. For those who prefer more freedom and flexibility, renting a car might be a good option, though it's more costly. Daily rental rates start at about €20, and fuel prices are reasonably comparable to the rest of Europe. However, travelers should be aware of parking costs in popular areas, as these can add up quickly.

Shopping for souvenirs and local goods can also vary in price. Markets and local shops offer unique items at reasonable prices, but it's always a good idea to compare shops and stalls to get the best deal. Remember that bargaining is not typically a part of Maltese culture, so the price you see is usually the final price. It's also wise to be prepared for other incidental costs such as entrance fees to museums, historical sites, and other attractions. These fees are generally modest but can range from a few Euros to around €10 or more for major sites.

Lastly, it's always a good idea to set aside a small amount of money for unexpected expenses, like tips in restaurants and cafes. Tipping is not mandatory in Malta, but it is appreciated for good service, typically around 10% of the bill.

By understanding the typical costs and budgeting accordingly, visitors can enjoy their stay in Malta without financial surprises, making the trip as enjoyable and stress-free as possible. This way, you can focus more on experiencing the rich culture, beautiful landscapes, and warm hospitality that Malta is known for.

Best Times to Visit

Choosing the best time to visit Malta depends largely on what you hope to get out of your trip. Malta's Mediterranean climate means hot summers and mild winters, making it a year-round destination, but each season offers different experiences that cater to various interests.

Spring (March to May) is often considered the ideal time to visit. The weather is pleasantly warm with average temperatures ranging from 15°C to 23°C (59°F to 73°F), making it comfortable for exploring the outdoors. The countryside is lush and green, wildflowers bloom, and the tourist crowds have not yet peaked, providing a more relaxed atmosphere. This season is perfect for sightseeing, hiking, and attending one of the many local festivals that begin in spring.

Summer (June to August) brings the peak tourist season to Malta, driven by hot, sunny weather with temperatures frequently climbing above

30°C (86°F). The seas are warm and ideal for swimming, snorkeling, and diving—one of Malta's signature activities. Summer is bustling with energy; the islands host numerous music festivals, outdoor concerts, and village feasts, known as 'festas', which celebrate local patron saints with processions, fireworks, and community gatherings. However, be prepared for higher prices and more crowded attractions during this time.

Autumn (September to November) sees a gradual decrease in temperatures and tourist numbers, making it another favorable season to visit. The weather remains warm enough to enjoy the beaches in early autumn, with temperatures ranging from 20°C to 28°C (68°F to 82°F). The sea also retains its summer warmth, extending the swimming season. This time of year is ideal for those interested in outdoor activities such as walking or cycling, especially as the landscape turns golden and the first rains refresh the arid summer scenery.

Winter (December to February) in Malta is mild compared to much of Europe, with temperatures rarely falling below 10°C (50°F). While it's the quietest tourist period, it's a great time for those looking to explore the cultural and historic sites without the crowds. Occasional rain showers occur, but they are usually short-lived, and many days remain sunny. Winter can be particularly appealing for those interested in a more laid-back experience or looking for a festive getaway, as Christmas and New Year are widely celebrated with unique local traditions and ample holiday spirit.

Each season in Malta offers a distinct set of advantages depending on your personal preferences, whether you're seeking outdoor adventure, cultural immersion, or simply a quiet escape. By understanding the seasonal variations, you can plan your visit to coincide with the activities and experiences that interest you most, ensuring a memorable and fulfilling journey to this vibrant archipelago.

Cultural Etiquette and Local Customs

Understanding the cultural etiquette and local customs of Malta is crucial for any visitor. This knowledge helps ensure respectful interactions and can enrich your travel experience by deepening your appreciation of the island's unique cultural identity.

Malta is a nation deeply rooted in tradition and strongly influenced by its history of religious devotion, which plays a significant role in daily life and social customs. One of the most prominent aspects of Maltese culture is the importance of family. Maltese families are typically close-knit, with strong bonds extending to wider family circles. When engaging with locals, showing respect for family values and inquiring about their well-being is appreciated.

Religion, particularly Roman Catholicism, is integral to Maltese culture. This is visible in the numerous churches and the religious festivals celebrated throughout the year. When visiting churches, dress modestly by covering your shoulders and knees. These sites are places of worship, so maintaining a quiet demeanor and showing reverence is expected. If you visit Malta during a religious festival, it's a wonderful opportunity to witness local traditions, but always be respectful, participate only where appropriate, and avoid disrupting the ceremonies.

In terms of greeting customs, Maltese people are generally warm and welcoming. A handshake is common when meeting someone for the first time. Once a relationship is established, it may be common to greet with a light kiss on both cheeks, particularly among women. When addressing someone, use titles and surnames until invited to use first names. This shows respect and is particularly important when interacting with older individuals.

When invited to a Maltese home, it is polite to bring a small gift, such as a dessert, flowers, or a bottle of wine. Arrive on time or slightly later than the agreed time—being extremely early is often considered as inconvenient as being late. During meals, observe your hosts for cues on when to start eating and follow their lead in social conversations.

Maltese people are known for their hospitality and often go out of their way to help tourists. When asking for directions or assistance, a polite "please" and "thank you" in English—widely spoken across the islands—will be well received. Tipping is customary in Malta, similar to other European countries. In restaurants, it's usual to leave a tip of around 10% of the bill if the service charge isn't included.

Lastly, Maltese society is relatively conservative, and public behavior should be courteous. Public displays of affection are fine but should be kept modest. Similarly, loud and raucous behavior is frowned upon, especially in quiet or religious neighborhoods.

By following these guidelines on cultural etiquette and local customs, you can show your respect for the Maltese people and their traditions. This not only makes your visit more pleasant but also opens up opportunities for genuine cultural exchange and a deeper understanding of this Mediterranean gem.

Language Basics

In Malta, language is a vivid tapestry of the island's history, with Maltese and English serving as the two official languages. This dual linguistic identity not only reflects Malta's complex past but also its modern European character, making communication for travelers typically straightforward and convenient.

Maltese, the national language, has its roots in Arabic but is heavily influenced by Italian, Sicilian, and English, making it a unique Semitic language written in the Latin script. For anyone keen to dive into the local culture, learning a few phrases in Maltese can be a delightful way to connect with the islanders, who appreciate the effort and are typically eager to help you learn.

English, stemming from Malta's period as a British colony, is widely spoken across the islands, used in government, commerce, and education, and is familiar to nearly all locals. This makes navigating, reading signs, menus, and accessing services relatively easy for English-speaking visitors.

For travelers interested in basic Maltese phrases, here are some to get started:
- **Hello:** "Merħba" (MER-hba)
- **Goodbye:** "Saħħa" (Sa-HA)
- **Please:** "Jekk jogħġbok" (Yekk yoh-JBOK)
- **Thank you:** "Grazzi" (GRUTS-zi)
- **Yes:** "Iva" (EE-va)
- **No:** "Le" (lay)
- **Excuse me / Sorry:** "Skużani" (skoo-ZAH-nee)

Learning these basics can enhance your interactions with locals, adding a layer of richness to your travels in Malta. Moreover, it demonstrates respect and interest in the Maltese culture, often leading to warmer receptions and enriching exchanges.

In restaurants, hotels, and other tourist spots, English is commonly used, making communication straightforward. However, in more rural areas or with older generations, you might find Maltese more prevalent. Here, having some knowledge of basic Maltese phrases can be particularly beneficial.

Malta also has a small community of Italian speakers, a legacy of its close proximity and historical ties to Italy. Italian media is popular and widely consumed, and you will find that many Maltese are proficient in Italian, adding another layer of linguistic diversity.

For anyone staying longer, or for those with a deeper interest in Malta's linguistic landscape, learning Maltese provides insights into the island's Semitic language heritage, which is quite unique within Europe. Maltese language courses are available for those who wish to delve deeper, and many find this a rewarding way to connect more profoundly with Malta's rich cultural tapestry.

Understanding and using the basics of the local language can greatly enhance your travel experience, making your interactions more meaningful and your journey through Malta more memorable.

CHAPTER 2

Getting There and Around

Arriving in Malta and navigating around the islands is an integral part of your travel experience. This chapter will guide you through the various options available for reaching Malta and moving around once you are here, ensuring you can plan your journey with ease.

Malta is accessible primarily through air and sea. Most visitors fly into Malta International Airport, the archipelago's only airport, which serves numerous airlines offering direct and connecting flights from Europe and other continents. Alternatively, traveling by sea is another option, with ferries arriving from several Mediterranean ports, adding a scenic route to your adventure.

Once in Malta, getting around is straightforward due to the small size of the islands. This chapter will explore the different modes of transportation available to tourists. We'll cover the public bus service, which is an economical and efficient way to travel across the main islands. For more flexibility, renting a car might be preferable, although driving in Malta comes with its own set of challenges such as left-hand traffic and sometimes narrow, winding roads. Other options include taxis, which are readily available, and the increasingly popular ride-sharing services.

We will also discuss tips for navigating by sea between the islands, using the regular ferry services that connect Malta, Gozo, and Comino, offering not just transport but also beautiful views of the Mediterranean. With the right information, getting to and around Malta can be an enjoyable part of your travel experience, allowing you to make the most of your visit without the stress of uncertain logistics. This chapter aims to equip you with all the knowledge needed to navigate Malta's landscapes smoothly and enjoyably.

How to Get There: Air and Sea Travel

Reaching Malta is a straightforward process, with options available through both air and sea travel, catering to visitors from near and far. This detailed guide will help you understand the best ways to arrive in Malta and start your adventure in this beautiful archipelago.

Air Travel

Malta International Airport (MLA) is the primary gateway for air travelers. Located between the towns of Luqa and Gudja, the airport is well connected and just a short drive from the capital, Valletta. It hosts a wide range of airlines, including national carriers and low-cost airlines, providing direct flights from major cities in Europe as well as connecting flights from other continents. Upon landing, you will find various amenities and services at the airport, such as car rental agencies, taxi services, and public transport connections that can take you to different parts of the island.

The frequency and availability of flights to Malta increase during the tourist season, from late spring to early autumn, reflecting the island's popularity as a summer destination. Booking your flight in advance during these peak times is advisable to secure the best rates and ensure availability.

Sea Travel

For those who prefer traveling by sea, Malta is serviced by several international ferry connections. The main port, the Grand Harbour, located in Valletta, is one of the most stunning natural harbors in Europe and a hub of maritime activity. Ferries and cruise ships regularly dock at this port, linking Malta with various Italian ports such as Catania and Genoa, and offering a scenic approach to the island. Regular ferries also operate between Malta and its sister island, Gozo. These ferries are frequent, affordable, and provide a vital link for both residents and tourists wishing to explore the distinct charm of Gozo. The short trip offers beautiful views of the Mediterranean and is a refreshing way to start your exploration of the Maltese Islands.

For a more luxurious or leisurely approach, considering a cruise might be ideal. The Mediterranean cruise routes often include a stop in Malta, allowing you to disembark and enjoy the island for a day or two before continuing on your journey. This option combines the convenience of multiple travel destinations with the comfort of a cruise ship. Whether arriving by air or sea, once you reach Malta, you will find an island ready to welcome you with its rich history, vibrant culture, and breathtaking landscapes. The ease of travel, coupled with the warm Maltese hospitality, ensures that your journey to Malta is as pleasant as your stay. Understanding these travel options allows you to choose the best route that suits your needs and preferences, setting the stage for a memorable visit to this unique Mediterranean destination.

Getting Around: Transportation Tips

Navigating Malta is an essential part of your travel experience, and understanding the various transportation options available can greatly enhance your visit. Malta may be a small island, but it offers a well-organized and efficient transportation network that caters to both locals and tourists, making it easy to explore its many attractions.

Public Buses

The bus service in Malta is the most common and cost-effective way to get around. The network is extensive, covering all major tourist destinations, towns, and villages. Buses in Malta are easily recognizable by their bright colors, and they operate regularly from early morning until late at night, including special night routes that serve main entertainment hubs. For tourists, purchasing a multi-day travel card can offer unlimited travel and is an economical choice compared to single tickets. Information on routes and timetables is readily available online, at bus stops, or through mobile apps dedicated to Maltese public transport.

Taxis and Ride-Sharing

Taxis are widely available in Malta and can be a convenient option for direct travel to specific destinations without the stops required on bus routes. They can be hailed on the street, booked via phone, or arranged through hotels. Additionally, ride-sharing services operate in Malta, providing an alternative to traditional taxis with easy booking through smartphone apps, offering transparent pricing and route details before you commit to the ride.

Car Rentals

Renting a car gives you the flexibility to travel at your own pace and on your own schedule. Car rental agencies are found at the airport, in major towns, and at tourist spots. While driving in Malta offers greater freedom, it's important to be mindful of the local driving conditions. Roads can be narrow and winding, especially in older towns and rural areas. Traffic drives on the left-hand side, as in the UK, which may require some adjustment for visitors from countries where right-hand driving is the norm. Parking in tourist areas can be challenging during peak seasons, so planning ahead for parking spots is advisable.

Ferries

For trips between the main island and the smaller islands of Gozo and Comino, ferries are an excellent and scenic option. The ferry service is regular and reliable, with schedules that cater to both residents and tourists. These ferries accommodate passengers and vehicles, making them a good option if you are renting a car and wish to explore multiple islands during your stay.

Bicycles and Scooters

For shorter distances or leisurely exploration, renting bicycles or scooters can be both enjoyable and environmentally friendly. Many coastal paths and promenades are well-suited for cycling, offering stunning views and a refreshing breeze off the Mediterranean. Some areas also offer dedicated bike lanes, enhancing safety for cyclists.

Understanding these options and choosing the right mode of transport can significantly influence your experience in Malta. Whether you prefer the independence of driving, the affordability of buses, or the convenience of taxis, Malta's transportation network supports a variety of preferences and needs, ensuring that you can explore this beautiful island with ease and comfort.

In addition, for car rentals in Malta, you have a range of options tailored to various travel needs and budgets. Here are a few recommendations:

1. Queen Car Rental
    - **Location:** Service provided at Malta International Airport and other locations by arrangement.
    - **Contact:** Specific contact details are available on their website.
    - **Website:** (https://queencarentalmalta.com/)
    - **Cost:** Prices vary depending on vehicle type and rental duration.

2. Finalrentals
    - **Location:** Offers pick-up and drop-off at various locations around Malta.
    - **Contact:** Interaction mainly through their website.
    - **Website:** (https://www.finalrentals.mt/)
    - **Cost:** Starting from around $37 per day for a standard vehicle.

These companies offer a variety of vehicles, from compact cars to SUVs, ensuring that you can find something that fits your needs whether you're planning a short stay or a longer exploration. They also provide detailed information on rental conditions, insurance options, and booking procedures on their websites.

For public transport, Malta has a comprehensive bus service operated by Malta Public Transport which covers the main tourist areas and extends to more remote locations. Prices for bus tickets are quite reasonable, with day passes available that offer unlimited travel.

- **Website:**(https://www.publictransport.com.mt/)
- **Cost:** A day pass costs around $2.24, offering great value for extensive travel across the island.

These services provide a reliable and cost-effective way to explore Malta's rich landscapes and cultural sites.

CHAPTER 3

Accommodation Options

Choosing the right place to stay is crucial to the enjoyment of your visit to Malta, and the islands offer a wide range of accommodation options to suit every taste and budget. This chapter will guide you through the diverse types of lodgings available, from the plush comfort of luxury hotels to the charm of budget-friendly options, ensuring you find the perfect base for your Maltese adventure.

For those looking for a touch of luxury, Malta boasts a number of high-end hotels that offer exquisite services and amenities. These establishments often provide stunning views, world-class dining, and extra services like spas and private tours. On the other end of the spectrum, budget hotels and hostels present clean and comfortable accommodations without the frills, perfect for travelers who prefer to spend their days exploring rather than staying indoors.

Delving deeper into Malta's unique offerings, you will discover boutique hotels and historic inns that blend rich history with modern luxury. These accommodations are often situated in beautifully restored buildings and offer a personal touch in their service, making your stay both memorable and intimate.

Families traveling with children will appreciate the array of family-friendly stays and resorts specifically designed to cater to the needs of both adults and young ones. These places often feature family rooms, children's activities, and facilities like pools and play areas to keep everyone entertained.

For a truly unique experience, consider staying in a traditional Maltese farmhouse or a heritage home. These accommodations provide a glimpse into the rustic charm and architectural tradition of Malta, offering a peaceful retreat in some of the island's most picturesque settings.

Finally, we will provide practical booking tips and recommend platforms to help you secure the best accommodation that fits your preferences and budget. Whether you are booking online or through a travel agent, understanding the best practices for reserving your stay in Malta can help you avoid pitfalls and ensure a smooth start to your holiday.

This chapter is designed to equip you with all the necessary information to make well-informed decisions on where to stay in Malta, enhancing your overall travel experience and allowing you to fully immerse yourself in the beauty and culture of the islands.

Hotels: From Luxury to Budget

In Malta, the range of hotel accommodations extends from opulent luxury to practical budget options, providing choices that cater to different preferences and financial plans. This spectrum ensures that every traveler can find a suitable place to stay, enhancing their experience of the island.

Luxury hotels in Malta are renowned for their exceptional service, extensive amenities, and often spectacular locations. These establishments typically offer spacious, elegantly furnished rooms with breathtaking views of the Mediterranean Sea or the historic cities of Valletta and Mdina. Guests can expect top-tier facilities such as on-site gourmet restaurants, private beaches, infinity pools, and comprehensive spa services. These hotels often provide concierge services to help guests arrange private tours, yacht charters, and other exclusive experiences. Staying at one of these hotels means not just a place to sleep, but a rich, immersive experience that can make your visit truly unforgettable.

Mid-range hotels strike a balance between comfort and cost, providing good quality accommodations without the expense of luxury amenities. These hotels usually feature clean, comfortable rooms, often with charming views and accessible services. Many mid-range hotels also offer facilities like swimming pools, on-site dining, and assistance with booking tours and transportation. They are ideal for travelers who appreciate comfort and convenience but do not require the lavish extras offered by more expensive establishments.

Budget hotels and hostels in Malta offer the most economical options for accommodations. These facilities prioritize basic comfort, cleanliness, and affordability. Rooms are typically more functional than luxurious, with simple furnishings and limited amenities. However, many budget hotels still provide essential services such as free Wi-Fi, breakfast, and travel advice. Hostels, in particular, are perfect for solo travelers, backpackers, or groups of friends looking to economize. They often have shared rooms and communal areas, which provide opportunities to meet other travelers. Budget accommodations are usually well-located, offering easy access to public transportation and local attractions, making them a practical base for exploring Malta.

When choosing a hotel in Malta, consider what is most important for your stay. Whether it's the indulgence of a luxury hotel, the balanced offer of a mid-range option, or the practicality of a budget hotel, Malta's range of accommodations has something to offer for every type of traveler.

Additionaly, when visiting Malta, choosing the right hotel can significantly enhance your stay. These recommendations cater to various tastes and budgets, ensuring every traveler finds a suitable accommodation.

Luxury Hotels

1. The Xara Palace Relais & Chateaux
- **Address:** Misrah il-Kunsill, Mdina, MDN 1050, Malta
- **Phone:** +356 2145 0560
- **Email:** info@xarapalace.com.mt
- **Website:**(https://www.xarapalace.com.mt)
- **Price Range:** $300 - $500 per night

Nestled in the medieval city of Mdina, The Xara Palace offers exclusive accommodations with panoramic views, gourmet dining, and a truly luxurious ambiance.

2. Hilton Malta
- **Address:** Portomaso, St. Julian's, PTM 01, Malta
- **Phone:** +356 2138 3383
- **Email:** info.malta@hilton.com

- **Website:** (https://www.hilton.com/en/hotels/mlahihi-hilton-malta/)
- **Price Range:** $250 - $450 per night

Situated in the vibrant area of St. Julian's, Hilton Malta features stylish rooms, multiple restaurants, a spa, several pools, and excellent service.

Mid-Range Hotels
1. Hotel Juliani
- **Address:** 25 St George's Rd, St Julian's STJ, 3208, Malta
- **Phone:** +356 2138 8000
- **Email:** reservations@hoteljuliani.com
- **Website:** (https://www.hoteljuliani.com)
- **Price Range:** $150 - $250 per night

A boutique hotel offering a rooftop pool and spectacular views of the bay, Hotel Juliani promises a comfortable stay with excellent amenities.

2. **Argento Hotel**
   - **Address:** Qaliet Street, St Julian's STJ 3255, Malta
   - **Phone:** +356 2138 8000
   - **Email:** info@hotelargento.com
   - **Website:** (https://www.hotelargento.com)
   - **Price Range:** $100 - $200 per night

   Located in the heart of St. Julian's, Argento Hotel provides modern comfort with easy access to the area's best attractions and dining options.

Budget Hotels

1. **Slimiza Suites**
   - **Address:** 29 Cathedral St, Sliema SLM1524, Malta
   - **Phone:** +356 2132 0001
   - **Email:** info@slimizasuites.com
   - **Website:** (https://www.slimizasuites.com)
   - **Price Range:** $50 - $100 per night

   A short walk from Sliema waterfront, Slimiza Suites offers clean, modern rooms at an affordable price, perfect for budget-conscious travelers.

2. Two Pillows Boutique Hostel
- **Address:** 49, Triq San Piju V, Sliema SLM1426, Malta
- **Phone:** +356 2731 2253
- **Email:** info@twopillowsmalta.com
- **Website:**(https://www.twopillowsmalta.com)
- **Price Range:** $20 - $80 per night

Ideal for backpackers and solo travelers, this boutique hostel in the heart of Sliema provides a cozy, communal atmosphere with both private rooms and dormitory options.

Each of these hotels offers distinct experiences, reflecting their respective categories. When booking, it's advisable to check current prices as they can fluctuate based on the season and availability. Whether you seek luxury, comfort, or economy, Malta's diverse accommodations are sure to meet your needs.

Boutique Hotels and Historic Inns

Boutique hotels and historic inns in Malta offer visitors a distinctive and intimate lodging experience that combines modern comforts with the charm and character of the past. These establishments are typically smaller than mainstream hotels, providing a more personalized service that allows guests to immerse themselves deeply in Malta's rich cultural heritage.

Boutique Hotels in Malta are known for their unique themes and bespoke services. Unlike larger hotel chains, these smaller settings often feature eclectic decor that reflects the local artistry and historical influences of the Maltese islands. Each room might be individually decorated, offering a different experience in each visit. Boutique hotels place a strong emphasis on hospitality and detail, ensuring that guests feel both welcomed and treasured. Many are located in restored buildings that have been carefully renovated to preserve original features while providing contemporary luxury. Guests can expect high-quality furnishings, exceptional dining options that often include local cuisine, and often, prime locations in the heart of Malta's most picturesque towns.

Historic Inns provide a window into the past, allowing guests to stay in buildings that have stood for centuries. These inns are often found in converted palazzos, forts, or townhouses, each with a story to tell. Staying in a historic inn is much like stepping back in time but with all the modern amenities. Thick stone walls, antique furniture, and traditional Maltese tiles add to the ambiance, creating an authentically historical atmosphere. Many historic inns are family-run, offering a warm, personal touch often missing in larger establishments. The owners are usually keen to share stories of the building's past, providing insights into the local history and culture.

Guests choosing to stay in boutique hotels or historic inns are treated not just to a place to sleep but to an experience. These accommodations are ideal for travelers seeking something beyond the ordinary, offering a deeper connection to the place they are visiting. Here, it's not just about luxury; it's about authenticity, charm, and a sense of place.

When selecting a boutique hotel or historic inn, consider what aspects of Maltese culture you want to experience. Are you interested in a seaside retreat with views of the Mediterranean, or would you prefer an urban escape in a centuries-old building within walking distance of major historical sites? Whatever your preference, these accommodations promise more than just a bed for the night—they offer a gateway to the past and a unique way to experience the local lifestyle.

Booking a stay in one of Malta's boutique hotels or historic inns involves researching to find a place that suits your style and interests. Look for reviews and ratings to ensure quality and service meet your expectations. These types of accommodations are perfect for those who value atmosphere, history, and personal attention over the predictability of more standard hotel offerings. Additional, Certainly! Adding recommendations to the overview of boutique hotels and historic inns in Malta will provide a more practical and useful guide. Here are some well-regarded options, each offering a unique experience that highlights Malta's charm and history:

Boutique Hotels

1. Palais Le Brun

- **Address:** 101, Old Bakery Street, Valletta, Malta
- **Phone:** +356 2124 8844
- **Email:** info@palaislebrun.com
- **Website:** (https://palaislebrun.com)
- **Price Range:** $150 - $300 per night

Nestled in the heart of Valletta, this luxurious boutique hotel is housed in an original baroque building that once belonged to a Knight of Malta. It offers a rooftop pool and stunning city views.

2. Casa Ellul
- **Address:** 81 Old Theatre Street, Valletta VLT 1429, Malta
- **Phone:** +356 2122 4433
- **Email:** info@casaellul.com
- **Website:** (https://www.casaellul.com)
- **Price Range:** $200 - $350 per night

Set in a Victorian-era building, Casa Ellul combines classical elegance with modern design, located right next to the Opera House in the cultural capital.

Historic Inns

1. The Xara Palace Relais & Chateaux
- **Address:** Misrah il-Kunsill, Mdina, MDN 1050, Malta
- **Phone:** +356 2145 0560

- **Email:** info@xarapalace.com.mt
- **Website:**(https://www.xarapalace.com.mt)
- **Price Range:** $300 - $500 per night

This exclusive 17th-century palace offers luxury accommodation with period pieces and original artworks, nestled in the medieval walls of the silent city of Mdina.

2. Hotel Castille
- **Address:** Castille Square, Valletta, VLT 1211, Malta
- **Phone:** +356 2124 3677
- **Email:** castille@hotelcastillemalta.com
- **Website:**(https://www.hotelcastillemalta.com)
- **Price Range:** $100 - $200 per night

A charming inn located in a 16th-century building in Valletta, offering panoramic views of the Grand Harbour from its rooftop restaurant.

Each of these properties provides a blend of traditional Maltese hospitality with distinctive features that promise a memorable stay. Whether you opt for the refined elegance of a boutique hotel or the historic allure of an inn, these accommodations reflect the rich cultural heritage and architectural beauty of Malta. Prices can vary based on the season, so it is recommended to check current rates and availability directly with the hotels. Booking ahead can also secure better rates and ensure that you get to experience these unique properties during your visit to Malta.

Family-Friendly Stays and Resorts

When planning a family vacation, finding the right accommodation that caters to both adults and children is essential. In Malta, a variety of family-friendly stays and resorts offer amenities and services designed to ensure that every member of the family has a comfortable and enjoyable experience. These accommodations not only provide a base for exploring the island but also ensure that staying in is just as fun.

Family-friendly hotels and resorts in Malta are equipped with a range of facilities to entertain children and provide convenience for parents. Such accommodations often feature children's pools, play areas, and clubs with organized activities that engage young minds and allow parents some downtime. These hotels also typically offer spacious family rooms or interconnected rooms that provide ample space and privacy.

Safety is a paramount concern for these establishments. Many are designed with child safety features such as gated pools, babyproofing services for rooms, and 24-hour security. Dining options at family-friendly accommodations in Malta cater to young palates with children's menus while also offering a variety of cuisine that appeals to adults.

In addition to these amenities, many family-oriented resorts provide additional services such as babysitting, which allows parents the opportunity to enjoy an evening out exploring Malta's rich culinary scene or historic sites. Some resorts also feature spa facilities, fitness centers, and private beaches, ensuring that relaxation is just as accessible as entertainment.

Educational activities are another hallmark of family-friendly stays in Malta. These may include cultural workshops, environmental talks, and historical tours that are tailored to be engaging and accessible for children. Such activities not only entertain but also enrich young travelers' experiences, making their vacation both fun and informative.

Transportation services are often provided by these accommodations, either through shuttle buses or assistance with renting a vehicle equipped with child safety seats. This service helps families explore Malta's attractions conveniently and safely.

Choosing the right family-friendly accommodation in Malta means considering the specific needs of your family. Whether it's proximity to major attractions, the availability of certain amenities, or dietary considerations, it's important to communicate these needs when booking your stay. This ensures that the resort or hotel can adequately prepare for your arrival and tailor their services to enhance your family's experience.

By selecting accommodations that are dedicated to making family stays as enjoyable and hassle-free as possible, you ensure that your trip to Malta will be a memorable adventure for every family member. From the moment you check in until you depart, these family-friendly resorts strive to create a welcoming and enriching environment, contributing significantly to the success of your family vacation.

In addition, here are some recommended family-friendly stays and resorts in Malta that cater specifically to the needs of families, providing facilities and services that enhance both comfort and enjoyment for all ages:

1. db Seabank Resort + Spa
- **Address:** Marfa Road, Mellieħa MLH 9063, Malta
- **Phone:** +356 2289 1000
- **Email:** seabank@dbhotelsresorts.com

- **Website:**(https://www.dbhotelsresorts.com/dbseabank/)
- **Price Range:** $150 - $300 per night

This all-inclusive resort is perfect for families, offering extensive buffet options, a large pool complex with a dedicated children's area, and entertainment programs for all ages.

2. Radisson Blu Resort & Spa, Malta Golden Sands

- **Address:** Golden Bay, Mellieha, MLH 5510, Malta
- **Phone:** +356 2356 1000
- **Email:** info.goldensands@radissonblu.com
- **Website:**(https://www.radissonhotels.com/en-us/hotels/radisson-blu-resort-spa-malta-golden-sands)
- **Price Range:** $200 - $400 per night

Situated on one of Malta's best beaches, this resort offers a blend of luxury and comfort with family rooms, kid-friendly activities, and direct beach access.

3. **InterContinental Malta**
   - **Address:** St George's Bay, St. Julians, STJ 3310, Malta
   - **Phone:** +356 2137 7600
   - **Email:** malta@ihg.com
   - **Website:**(https://malta.intercontinental.com/)
   - **Price Range:** $180 - $350 per night

   With a dedicated kids' club, large family rooms, and multiple dining options, this hotel offers a luxury stay for families looking to explore the vibrant area of St. Julian's.

4. **Holiday Inn Express Malta**
   - **Address:** St George's Bay, St. Julian's, STJ 3310, Malta
   - **Phone:** +356 2339 5000
   - **Email:** hiexmalta@ihg.com
   - **Website:**(https://www.ihg.com/holidayinnexpress/hotels/us/en/st-julian's/mlahi/hoteldetail)

- **Price Range:** $100 - $200 per night

Centrally located in St. Julian's, this hotel provides comfort and convenience with family-friendly amenities at a more affordable price point, making it ideal for budget-conscious families.

Each of these properties offers different experiences but all prioritize making family stays comfortable and enjoyable with facilities designed for children and services that cater to the needs of all family members. Prices may vary by season and availability, so it's advisable to book early, especially during peak travel times like summer and holidays, to secure the best rates and ensure availability.

Unique Accommodations: Farmhouses and Heritage Homes

Exploring Malta's unique accommodations, such as traditional farmhouses and heritage homes, offers travelers an extraordinary way to experience the island's rich history and vibrant culture. These accommodations are not just places to stay but are gateways to understanding the Maltese way of life, blending the rustic charm of the past with modern comforts.

Traditional Farmhouses

Farmhouses in Malta are a testament to the island's agricultural past. Typically located in rural areas, these properties offer a tranquil retreat from the more tourist-centric locations. Maltese farmhouses are built with limestone, a material that naturally keeps the interiors cool in the hot Mediterranean summers. Many of these farmhouses have been thoughtfully restored to provide all the modern amenities while preserving their original character and rustic charm. Features often include thick stone walls, wooden beams, and courtyards or gardens with native plants.

These farmhouses commonly come equipped with kitchens, making them ideal for families or groups who prefer a self-catering option. They often feature outdoor areas with swimming pools, barbeque facilities, and ample space for dining al fresco under the stars. Staying in a farmhouse offers a peaceful experience, where one can enjoy the slow pace of island life surrounded by nature and history.

Heritage Homes

Heritage homes in Malta are another unique accommodation option, often found in urban settings like the historic cities of Valletta, Mdina, and Birgu. These residences are part of Malta's architectural heritage, many dating back to the time of the Knights of St. John. Staying in a heritage home is like living in a piece of history, each room and hall echoing stories of the past.

These homes are distinguished by architectural features such as baroque facades, traditional Maltese balconies, and intricate tile work. Inside, they are usually decorated to reflect the rich cultural heritage, with antique furniture, artworks, and tapestries. Modern renovations provide comfort without detracting from the historical integrity, offering amenities like Wi-Fi, modern bathrooms, and updated bedding.

Heritage homes can range from small, intimate lodgings perfect for couples to larger properties that can accommodate families or groups. They are particularly popular among travelers who seek a deeper cultural experience, offering a base that feels like a home away from home, steeped in local tradition and elegance.

Choosing Your Stay

When choosing a farmhouse or heritage home in Malta, consider what kind of experience you are looking for. If solitude and nature are your priorities, a farmhouse in the countryside might be ideal. If you prefer to be close to museums, restaurants, and historical sites, then a heritage home in one of Malta's storied cities could be the perfect fit.

These unique accommodations provide more than just a place to sleep; they offer an immersive experience into the Maltese lifestyle. Whether you opt for the rustic elegance of a farmhouse or the historical splendor of a heritage home, you will gain a deeper appreciation for Malta's rich history and vibrant present.

In addition, here are some recommended unique accommodations in Malta, including traditional farmhouses and heritage homes. Each offers a distinct experience that showcases the local architecture and history, providing an immersive stay in the heart of Malta's culture.

Farmhouses

1. Ta' Mena Estate

- **Address:** Rabat Road, Xaghra, Gozo, Malta
- **Phone:** +356 2156 4939
- **Email:** info@tamena-gozo.com
- **Website:** (http://www.tamena-gozo.com)
- **Price Range:** $120 - $250 per night

Nestled in the beautiful island of Gozo, Ta' Mena Estate offers a rustic stay with modern amenities, surrounded by vineyards and orchards, perfect for a tranquil retreat.

2. Razzett Bardan

- **Address:** Lighthouse Street, Ghasri, Gozo, Malta
- **Phone:** +356 9928 0000
- **Email:** contact@gozofarmhouses.com
- **Website:** (https://www.gozofarmhouses.com)
- **Price Range:** $100 - $220 per night

This beautifully converted farmhouse combines rustic charm with luxury, featuring a private pool, sun terraces, and stunning countryside views.

Heritage Homes

1. Palazzo Consiglia
- **Address:** 102, St. Ursula Street, Valletta, Malta
- **Phone:** +356 2124 4222
- **Email:** info@palazzoconsiglia.com
- **Website:** (https://palazzoconsiglia.com)
- **Price Range:** $180 - $350 per night

Located in the historic heart of Valletta, this traditional Maltese townhouse has been transformed into a luxurious boutique hotel, maintaining all its period features with an added touch of modern comfort.

2. The Coleridge
- **Address:** 89, Old Bakery Street, Valletta, Malta
- **Phone:** +356 2713 0000

- **Email:** stay@thecoleridge.com
- **Website:** (https://thecoleridge.com)
- **Price Range:** $150 - $300 per night

A small boutique hotel in a carefully restored 17th-century building, offering a blend of historic charm and contemporary elegance in the cultural epicenter of Malta.

Each of these accommodations provides guests with more than just a place to stay—they offer a portal into the traditional Maltese way of life. Whether you choose the pastoral beauty of a Gozo farmhouse or the rich history of a Valletta heritage home, these properties promise a memorable and enriching stay in Malta.

Booking Tips and Recommended Platforms

Booking accommodations in Malta can be a straightforward process if you know the right tips and platforms to use. Whether you're looking for a luxurious hotel, a cozy bed and breakfast, or a unique farmhouse stay, understanding how to navigate the booking process will help you secure the best options to suit your travel needs and budget.

Start Early: Especially during peak tourist seasons, Malta's most desirable accommodations can get booked quickly. Starting your search early gives you a broader selection of options and often better prices. For summer travel, consider booking your stay as early as possible—sometimes six months in advance. For less busy seasons, booking a few months ahead should suffice.

Use Reliable Booking Platforms: There are several reputable online booking platforms that offer a wide range of accommodations in Malta. Platforms like Booking.com, Airbnb, and Expedia are widely used and provide user reviews, which can help you make informed decisions. These sites also offer detailed descriptions, photos, and maps, making it easier to find accommodations that match your preferences in terms of location, amenities, and price.

Compare Prices: Don't book the first option you find. Spend some time comparing prices and what each accommodation offers. Sometimes, booking directly through a hotel's or property's own website can offer lower rates than those found on large booking platforms. Additionally, some sites may have special deals or packages that include additional benefits like free breakfast, parking, or Wi-Fi.

Read Reviews: Reviews from previous guests are invaluable when choosing where to stay. They provide insight into the quality of the rooms, the friendliness of the staff, the convenience of the location, and much more. Pay attention to recurring comments, both positive and negative. This feedback can give you a realistic expectation of what to expect and help you avoid places that might not meet your standards.

Consider Travel Packages: Sometimes, you can find packages that include not just accommodations but also transportation, meals, or even tours and activities. Travel agencies or even some booking platforms might offer these packages at a competitive rate, which could save you money and time in planning logistics.

Understand the Cancellation Policy: Before finalizing any booking, always check the cancellation policy. This is crucial if your plans are subject to change. Some bookings offer free cancellation within a certain period, while others might be non-refundable. Understanding these policies can save you from unexpected charges if you need to alter your plans.

Contact the Property for Special Requests: If you have specific needs such as a late check-in, dietary restrictions, or need amenities like a crib for a baby, it's a good idea to contact the property directly before booking. This ensures they can accommodate your needs and also helps avoid any surprises during your stay.

By following these tips and using recommended platforms, you can streamline your booking process, secure accommodations that cater perfectly to your preferences, and even snag some great deals. Remember, the key to a successful booking experience is research, comparison, and planning ahead—this ensures you have the most enjoyable and stress-free stay in Malta.

CHAPTER 4

Culinary and Dining Experience

Embarking on a culinary journey through Malta offers an enriching insight into the island's culture, history, and traditions. Maltese cuisine is a delightful tapestry woven from the various civilizations that have inhabited the island, including influences from Sicilian, Middle Eastern, and British kitchens. This chapter will guide you through a mouth-watering exploration of what makes Maltese dining truly unique.

We will start by delving into the heart of Maltese gastronomy with a look at local cuisine and must-try dishes. From the robust flavors of traditional rabbit stew, known as 'stuffat tal-fenek', to the crispy, savory pastizzi, you'll learn about the foods that are staples in every Maltese kitchen. These dishes not only provide sustenance but also carry the stories and practices of the people who make up Malta's vibrant community.

Next, we will navigate through the top restaurants across Malta that are acclaimed for their culinary excellence. Whether you're seeking a luxurious dining experience by the sea or a charming eatery tucked away in a narrow street of Valletta, this guide will help you discover the best places to savor authentic Maltese flavors as well as innovative cuisine that showcases the creativity of local chefs.

Lastly, for those who wish to dive deeper into the culinary arts of Malta, we will explore opportunities for cooking classes and culinary tours. These experiences allow you to not just taste but also create dishes using traditional techniques and local ingredients under the guidance of skilled chefs. It's a hands-on way to connect with Maltese culture and bring some of the flavors home with you.

This chapter promises to be a feast for the senses, offering everything from insights into daily Maltese dishes to exclusive dining experiences. It will not only guide your palate through an array of flavors but also deepen your appreciation for Malta's culinary heritage. Join us as we savor every bite and sip of this Mediterranean gem.

Local Cuisine and Must-Try Dishes

Malta's local cuisine is a rich blend of flavors influenced by the various cultures that have occupied the island over centuries. This unique culinary tradition is deeply rooted in the agrarian lifestyle of the Maltese people and the bountiful Mediterranean Sea that surrounds them. Here, we will explore some of the must-try dishes that embody the essence of Maltese cooking, offering a taste of the island's history and its people's way of life.

Fenkata (Rabbit Stew): This is the national dish of Malta, deeply embedded in local tradition. Fenkata involves a slow-cooked stew of rabbit, often marinated in wine or vinegar and seasoned with garlic, bay leaves, and other herbs. This dish is usually served during festive gatherings and is a true taste of Maltese communal life.

Pastizzi: These are savory pastries that are iconic in Maltese street food culture. Made from flaky, buttery pastry and filled with ricotta or a pea paste, pastizzi are perfect for a quick snack any time of the day. They're inexpensive and widely available from street vendors and cafes throughout the islands.

Bragioli (Beef Olives): Bragioli are beef slices stuffed with a mixture of minced meat, eggs, and herbs, then rolled, tied, and slow-cooked in a rich tomato sauce. This dish exemplifies the resourcefulness of traditional Maltese cooking, turning simple ingredients into a delicious and hearty meal.

Stuffat Tal-Qarnit (Octopus Stew): Reflecting Malta's island status, this octopus stew is a staple in the local diet. The octopus is cooked until tender with tomatoes, onions, olives, capers, and a dash of red wine, offering a succulent dish that captures the flavors of the Mediterranean Sea.

Ħobż biż-żejt: This is a traditional Maltese snack or light meal, consisting of a thick slice of Maltese bread rubbed with ripe tomatoes and topped with a mix of tuna, onions, garlic, and capers, all drizzled with olive oil. It's a simple yet flavorful dish that showcases the quality of local produce.

Imqaret (Date Pastries): These date-stuffed pastries are a favorite among Maltese sweets. Imqaret are made from a dough infused with aniseed and deep-fried until golden. Typically served warm, often with a scoop of ice cream, these treats are commonly found at local festivals and street markets.

Gbejniet (Maltese Cheese): This small, round cheese is made from goat's or sheep's milk. It can be served fresh, dried, or peppered with herbs and is a staple in Maltese kitchens, used in various dishes or enjoyed on its own, perhaps with a drizzle of local honey.

These dishes are not just meals; they are a window into the soul of Malta. They tell stories of familial bonds, community celebrations, and the islands' adaptations to the changing tides of history. Sampling these dishes provides not only a culinary delight but also a deeper understanding of the Maltese way of life. Whether dining in a local village eatery, a seaside restaurant, or trying your hand at cooking these dishes in a culinary class, each bite offers a connection to the rich tapestry that is Malta.

Top Restaurants Across Malta

Malta offers a rich dining landscape that mirrors its cultural diversity and historical layers. Across the islands, top restaurants showcase not only traditional Maltese dishes but also international cuisines, making Malta a vibrant culinary destination. Whether you're looking for a luxurious dining experience by the sea or a quaint eatery tucked away in a narrow alley, Malta's restaurants cater to every palate and occasion.

Fine Dining and Michelin-Starred Restaurants

Malta's fine dining scene has blossomed, with several restaurants earning Michelin stars for their outstanding cuisine and service. These establishments typically offer a gourmet experience that highlights fresh, local ingredients prepared with international culinary techniques.

- Under Grain, located in Valletta, is one of the Michelin-starred restaurants where elegance meets precision in cuisine. The restaurant offers a refined atmosphere with dishes that are as visually appealing as they are flavorful, often featuring local seafood and seasonal produce.

- De Mondion, set in Mdina, combines panoramic views of the island with a luxurious dining experience. Also boasting a Michelin star, De Mondion serves sophisticated Mediterranean dishes, focusing on quality and creativity.

Casual Dining and Traditional Eateries

For those seeking a more laid-back dining experience that reflects the hearty, rustic nature of Maltese cooking, there are numerous bistros and trattorias spread across the island that serve traditional fare.

- Ta' Kris Restaurant in Sliema is a local favorite, housed in a former bakery. It offers Maltese cuisine with a home-cooked feel, specializing in dishes like bragioli, lampuki pie (fish pie), and rabbit stew.

- Il-Kartell Restaurant, located by the sea in Marsalforn, Gozo, provides a picturesque setting to enjoy fresh seafood, from fish to squid, cooked in a myriad of local styles.

Vegetarian and Vegan Options

As global culinary trends evolve, Maltese restaurants are also embracing vegetarian and vegan menus to cater to all dietary preferences.

- Soul Food, located in Valletta, offers creative vegetarian and vegan dishes that use local, seasonal ingredients to produce flavorful and satisfying meals.

Street Food and Casual Snacks

For those exploring Malta's streets and historical sites, the local pastizzerias and cafes are perfect for grabbing a quick bite.

- Crystal Palace in Rabat is famous for its pastizzi, offering these flaky pastries filled with ricotta or peas at all hours, making it a must-visit for an authentic taste of Maltese street food.

Booking Tips

When planning to dine in Malta's top restaurants, especially the fine dining ones, it's advisable to book in advance, particularly during peak tourist seasons. Many restaurants have online booking systems, making it easy to secure a reservation. Checking restaurant reviews on platforms such as TripAdvisor or Google Reviews can also provide insights into the dining experience and help in making informed choices.

Dining in Malta can be as diverse and enriching as the island's history. From high-end restaurants that showcase the best of culinary sophistication to modest eateries that offer a taste of traditional

Maltese hospitality, the culinary scene is a testament to the island's rich cultural tapestry. Whether you are indulging in a sumptuous meal overlooking the Mediterranean or enjoying a quick pastizz at a local cafe, each meal is a reflection of Malta's heritage and its contemporary zest.

Cooking Classes and Culinary Tours

Engaging in cooking classes and culinary tours in Malta is an enriching way to delve deeper into the island's culture through its cuisine. These activities provide hands-on experiences that not only teach you how to prepare traditional Maltese dishes but also offer insights into the local way of life, history, and culinary traditions.

Cooking Classes in Malta

Cooking classes in Malta are a fantastic opportunity for food enthusiasts to learn directly from local chefs. These classes often take place in well-equipped kitchens that provide a welcoming and informative environment for learning. Participants are typically involved in every step of the cooking process, from selecting ingredients to the final preparation of dishes.

These cooking sessions may focus on a variety of traditional Maltese dishes such as Lampuki Pie (fish pie), Stuffat Tal-Qarnit (octopus stew), and

Timpana (baked pasta). More than just teaching recipes, these classes often delve into the history of Maltese cuisine and how it has been influenced by various Mediterranean cultures. This educational aspect makes the cooking experience more meaningful, as it ties the food to its cultural roots.

Culinary Tours in Malta

Culinary tours complement cooking classes by offering guided excursions that explore Malta's food scene. These tours can vary widely but typically include visits to local markets, traditional bakeries, and small-scale producers. Participants get to taste a variety of foods directly from the source, such as fresh seafood, artisan cheeses, and homemade wines.

One of the highlights of these tours is often a visit to a local market where tour guides explain how to choose the best ingredients and introduce the group to local vendors. This interaction not only supports local businesses but also helps participants understand the importance of each ingredient in Maltese cooking.

Wine Tasting Tours

Given Malta's growing reputation for wine production, many culinary tours include visits to local vineyards and wineries where traditional methods and modern techniques meet. These tours offer tastings of both red and white Maltese wines, which are gaining international recognition for their quality. The winery visits often come with discussions about grape cultivation on the islands and the wine-making process, offering a comprehensive look at the wine industry in Malta.

Booking a Cooking Class or Culinary Tour

When choosing a cooking class or culinary tour in Malta, it's important to consider what kind of experience you're looking for. Some classes and tours offer a more traditional approach focusing on Maltese classics, while others might incorporate contemporary techniques and international dishes.

It's advisable to book these activities in advance, especially during peak tourist seasons, to ensure availability. Many hotels and tourist information centers can provide recommendations and help with bookings. Online platforms also offer reviews and bookings for various culinary experiences, allowing you to see what previous participants have said about their experiences.

Overall, participating in cooking classes and culinary tours in Malta not only enhances your travel experience but also deepens your appreciation for Maltese culture. These activities are not just about food preparation; they are a celebration of Malta's heritage, a way to preserve traditional cooking methods, and an opportunity to understand the local lifestyle through its flavors and culinary practices.

In addition, here are some well-recommended cooking classes and culinary tours in Malta, each providing a unique insight into the local cuisine and culinary heritage. These experiences are designed to immerse participants fully into the Maltese food culture, offering both practical cooking skills and a deeper understanding of the island's gastronomy.

Cooking Classes

1. Maltese Mama Cooking Classes
- **Address:** St. Julian's, Malta
- **Phone:** +356 9901 4846
- **Email:** info@maltesemama.com
- **Website:** (http://www.maltesemama.com)
- **Price Range:** $50 - $100 per person

Experience the warmth of Maltese hospitality through these intimate cooking classes hosted in a traditional Maltese home. Learn to cook authentic Maltese dishes from an experienced local chef.

2. Sue's Cooking Classes

- **Address:** Sue's Kitchen, Triq il-Kbira, Mellieħa, Malta
- **Phone:** +356 9986 3327
- **Email:** sue@maltesecookingclass.com
- **Website:** (https://www.sueskitchenmalta.com)
- **Price Range:** $60 - $120 per person

Join Sue in her kitchen for a hands-on cooking experience where you'll prepare and enjoy traditional Maltese dishes, using fresh, seasonal ingredients from the local market.

Culinary Tours

1. Merill Eco Tours

- **Address:** Various locations around Malta and Gozo
- **Phone:** +356 9942 2256
- **Email:** info@merillecotours.com
- **Website:** (http://www.merillecotours.com)
- **Price Range:** $45 - $90 per person

Explore rural Malta with a guide who will take you through the local farms and artisan food producers. Taste organic and traditional foods and learn about sustainable agricultural practices in Malta.

2. Offbeat Malta Food Trails
- **Address:** Valletta, Malta
- **Phone:** +356 7906 2455
- **Email:** foodtrails@offbeatmalta.com
- **Website:**(https://offbeatmaltafoodtrails.com)
- **Price Range:** $55 - $100 per person

Dive into Malta's food scene with a guided tour around Valletta's eateries, bakeries, and markets. Enjoy tastings that include everything from street food to gourmet offerings.

These recommendations offer a mix of traditional and modern culinary experiences, suitable for everyone from serious food enthusiasts to casual cooks looking for a fun activity. Whether you opt for a cooking class to refine your culinary skills or a food trail to explore Malta's local flavors, each experience will add a rich layer to your visit to the islands. It's advisable to book these activities in advance as they tend to fill up quickly, especially during peak tourist seasons.

CHAPTER 5

Shopping and Souvenirs

Exploring the vibrant shopping scene in Malta offers tourists a delightful opportunity to discover unique products that reflect the island's rich culture and artisanal heritage. This chapter will guide you through various shopping experiences, from bustling markets and quaint street vendors to exclusive boutiques and specialty shops found in the historic cities of Valletta and Mdina.

As you traverse Malta's diverse shopping landscapes, you will encounter traditional markets brimming with fresh produce, local delicacies, and handmade goods. These markets are not only places to shop but are also vibrant cultural hubs where you can interact with local artisans and vendors, gaining insights into Maltese daily life and customs. In the elegant streets of Valletta and the medieval passages of Mdina, boutique shopping offers a different allure. Here, you can browse through high-end shops that showcase both international brands and local designs. These boutiques often house unique fashion items, offering a blend of contemporary style and traditional Maltese craftsmanship.

Souvenir shopping in Malta goes beyond the typical. It invites you to bring home pieces of Malta's heritage, such as intricately crafted lace, hand-painted ceramics, and filigree jewelry. Each of these items tells a story of Malta's artisanal traditions and serves as a lasting memento of your visit. Throughout this chapter, we will delve into the best places to discover these treasures, providing tips on where to find quality items and how to choose authentic Maltese handicrafts. Whether you are a casual shopper or a dedicated collector, Malta's shopping scene promises a rewarding and enriching experience, blending the joy of discovery with the pleasure of buying something truly unique.

Markets and Street Vendors

Exploring the markets and engaging with street vendors in Malta offers an authentic glimpse into the island's vibrant cultural and commercial life. Among the most notable is the Marsaxlokk Market located in the traditional fishing village of Marsaxlokk on Malta's southeastern coast. Renowned for its Sunday fish market, local fishermen sell the freshest catch alongside stalls brimming with traditional Maltese lace, handmade crafts, and an array of souvenirs. The market is easily accessible by a 30-minute bus ride from Valletta, and for those driving or taking a taxi, there is ample parking near the waterfront. A stroll along the picturesque waterfront lined with colorful traditional boats called luzzus is essential. Dining at one of the many seafood restaurants offers a taste of freshly caught seafood prepared in traditional Maltese styles, enhancing the market visit.

In the heart of Malta's capital, Valletta's Open Market, or Monti, operates daily around Merchant Street. This bustling market offers everything from affordable clothing to household goods and traditional Maltese food items. Centrally located, the market is a short walk from any part of the capital and easily reached by buses running from major towns. Exploring the market can be perfectly combined with visits to nearby historical sites like St. John's Co-Cathedral and the Grandmaster's Palace, with opportunities to sample local delicacies at nearby cafés.

Another significant market is the Ta' Qali Farmers Market, held every Tuesday and Saturday morning in the central part of Malta. Known for its fresh local produce sold directly by farmers, it features a vibrant selection of fruits, vegetables, cheeses, and honey. Although best accessed by car or taxi due to its rural setting, buses from Valletta and other towns also service this area. This market offers a chance to interact directly with local farmers, gaining insight into Maltese agricultural practices. Nearby, the Ta' Qali Crafts Village showcases local artisans at work, making it a perfect complement to the market visit.

When visiting these Maltese markets, it's wise to arrive early to avoid the crowds and heat of midday. This also ensures the best selection of products. Carrying cash is essential as many vendors do not accept cards, and haggling over prices is common. Engaging with vendors not only makes the shopping experience more enriching but also opens up conversations that reveal more about Maltese culture and traditions. Through these interactions and the variety of products available, visiting Maltese markets and street vendors becomes more than a shopping trip—it becomes a deep dive into the daily lives and traditions of the Maltese people, offering memories that are as lasting as the goods purchased.

Boutique Shopping in Valletta and Mdina

Boutique shopping in Valletta and Mdina offers visitors a unique blend of historical ambiance and contemporary retail experience. These two cities, rich in history and culture, are the epicenters for finding one-of-a-kind items ranging from high-end fashion to bespoke artisan products.

Valletta, the capital of Malta, is a UNESCO World Heritage site and provides a stunning backdrop for a shopping adventure. The city's main retail thoroughfares are Republic Street and Merchants Street. Here, shoppers can explore a variety of boutique shops offering everything from luxury brands to handcrafted Maltese jewelry and glassware. The compact nature of Valletta makes it easy to navigate on foot, and its grid-like layout ensures that visitors can enjoy a seamless shopping experience amidst the baroque architecture of the city.

Getting to Valletta is straightforward. It is well-connected by public transport from all major areas of Malta. Buses frequently run to Valletta and there is a central bus terminal on the outskirts of the city, making access convenient from anywhere on the island. For those driving, there are several parking areas at the city's entrance, although parking within the city is limited.

Aside from shopping, Valletta offers numerous cafes, museums, and historic sites. A visit to St. John's Co-Cathedral, with its opulent interior, or the Upper Barrakka Gardens for a panoramic view of the Grand Harbour, complements a day of shopping perfectly. These attractions enrich the experience, allowing visitors to immerse themselves not only in local commerce but also in the rich tapestry of Maltese history and art.

Mdina, the old capital, known as the "Silent City," offers a different ambiance. This walled city is pedestrian-only and known for its medieval and baroque architecture. Boutique shops in Mdina are more focused on artisan products such as hand-made lace, traditional Maltese filigree, and unique souvenirs that reflect the ancient history of the place. The narrow, winding streets of Mdina themselves make shopping here a unique experience, as each turn brings you face to face with centuries-old buildings and the chance to discover hidden boutiques.

Reaching Mdina is also easy by public transport, with direct buses available from Valletta and other major locations. For visitors driving, parking is available outside the city walls.

In Mdina, apart from shopping, visitors should not miss the opportunity to visit St. Paul's Cathedral or the Mdina Dungeons. A walk along the bastions provides breathtaking views of the island. Dining in Mdina, especially at the famed Fontanella Tea Garden, which offers delicious cakes with a view, or at one of the fine dining restaurants tucked away in ancient palazzos, should be part of your visit.

Both Valletta and Mdina offer more than just shopping; they provide a cultural experience that includes history, architecture, and gastronomy, making any visit a multifaceted discovery. Whether you are looking for the latest fashion, searching for a unique gift, or simply soaking up the atmosphere of these ancient cities, boutique shopping in Valletta and Mdina is sure to leave a lasting impression.

Souvenir Shopping: Local Handicrafts and Unique Finds

Souvenir shopping in Malta offers visitors a chance to take home a piece of the island's rich cultural heritage. The Maltese islands are renowned for their artisanal crafts, which are deeply rooted in centuries-old traditions. From the intricate lacework of Gozo to the unique filigree silverwork, each handmade item tells a story of Malta's history and the skilled craftsmanship of its people.

One of the most cherished Maltese handicrafts is lace-making, known locally as 'bizzilla.' This delicate craft was introduced to Malta in the 16th century and has since evolved into a symbol of Maltese cultural identity. The town of Gozo, in particular, is famous for its lace; visitors can find everything from traditional tablecloths to contemporary fashion items adorned with lace. Shopping for these lace products not only supports local artisans but also helps preserve this age-old craft for future generations.

Another notable Maltese handicraft is filigree silverwork. This involves twisting thin silver threads into intricate designs to create exquisite jewelry and decorative items. The technique demands a high level of precision and artistry, making each piece a unique work of art. Maltese filigree is highly prized and makes for an elegant and timeless souvenir.

In addition to lace and filigree, Malta is also known for its hand-painted ceramics and blown glass. These vibrant crafts reflect the colors and spirit of the Mediterranean. The town of Ta' Qali is home to several artisans who specialize in these crafts. Visitors can often watch these skilled craftsmen at work, blowing glass into beautiful shapes or painting detailed designs onto pottery, offering an insight into the creative process behind these beautiful creations.

When it comes to buying these handicrafts, several locations across the islands cater to those looking for authentic Maltese souvenirs. The Ta' Qali Crafts Village is a popular spot where tourists can purchase directly from artisans. Here, one can explore numerous workshops and boutiques, each offering a variety of handmade products that showcase Maltese craftsmanship.

For those visiting the capital, Valletta offers numerous shops specializing in local handicrafts. These shops are typically located along the main streets and within the city's bustling marketplaces. Shopping in these areas provides a lively experience where one can soak in the local atmosphere and perhaps even haggle to get a better deal.

Beyond tangible goods, souvenir shopping in Malta is also about the experiences and memories that come with interacting with local artisans.

Many shoppers find that the stories behind their purchases—how they were made, or the history of the craft—add immeasurable value to the items themselves. These stories can transform a simple object into a treasured keepsake that carries with it the essence of Malta.

In essence, souvenir shopping in Malta is not just about acquiring items to remember your trip; it's an exploration of Malta's cultural fabric, an opportunity to engage with the island's heritage and traditions. Whether you're browsing lace in Gozo, admiring filigree in Valletta, or watching glass-blowers in Ta' Qali, the experience is sure to enrich your understanding of this unique Mediterranean culture.

CHAPTER 6

Top Attractions and Activities

Malta, a jewel in the heart of the Mediterranean, offers a tapestry of experiences that blend its rich history with stunning natural beauty. This chapter will guide you through the top attractions and activities that make Malta a unique destination for any traveler. From the historical and cultural richness of Valletta to the serene landscapes of Gozo, each site and activity provides a window into the soul of this captivating island nation.

In Valletta, Malta's capital, you are invited to explore a city steeped in history, where ancient walls and narrow streets tell stories of knights and sieges. Key attractions such as St. John's Co-Cathedral, with its opulent interior, and the Lascaris War Rooms, an underground complex that played a pivotal role during World War II, offer insights into Malta's strategic importance through the ages. The Upper & Lower Barrakka Gardens provide not only a peaceful retreat but also panoramic views of the historic Grand Harbour.

Beyond the capital, the museums distributed across the island—including the National War Museum, the National Archaeology Museum, and the Malta at War Museum—serve as custodians of Malta's legacy, displaying artifacts that span thousands of years, from prehistory to modern times.

A short ferry ride from Malta, Gozo, the island sanctuary, awaits with its more tranquil pace and picturesque landscapes. Here, historical sites like the Ggantija Temples, some of the oldest free-standing structures in the world, and The Old Prison in Victoria's citadel, offer a glimpse into Gozo's past. The island's natural beauty is on full display at locations such as Ta' Cenc Cliffs and

Ninu's Cave, which offer stunning vistas and opportunities for quiet reflection.

Gozo is also home to significant cultural institutions such as the Gozo Archaeology Museum and the Gozo Cathedral Museum, each showcasing the rich cultural heritage and artistic achievements of the island.

This chapter will not only introduce you to these incredible sites and activities but also provide practical advice on how best to experience them, enhancing your journey through Malta's history, culture, and landscapes. Whether you are meandering through the bustling streets of Valletta, delving into the ancient history of Gozo, or simply soaking in the natural beauty that abounds, your time in Malta is sure to be filled with discovery and delight.

History and Culture of Valletta

Valletta, the capital of Malta, is a city steeped in history and culture, richly deserving of its title as a UNESCO World Heritage site. Founded in 1566 by Jean Parisot de la Valette, the Grand Master of the Order of St. John, Valletta was built as a fortress to defend against Ottoman invasions after the Great Siege of Malta. Its strategic importance was unparalleled, standing as the key to control over the central Mediterranean.

The city's layout is a testament to its Renaissance origins, characterized by a grid-like street system that was revolutionary at the time. This design not only facilitated movement and defense but also provided the city with a sense of order and modernity that was rare during this period. The streets of Valletta are lined with Baroque architecture, majestic palaces, and imposing churches, each telling a story of a past era. The most iconic of these is St. John's Co-Cathedral, with its lavish interior adorned by Mattia Preti and its floor composed of marble tombstones of the Knights of St. John, reflecting the opulence and power of the Order. Valletta's cultural landscape is as rich as its history. The city has been a hub of activity and administration for centuries, undergoing various periods of development under the Knights of St. John, the French under Napoleon, and the British, before becoming the capital of independent Malta in 1964. Each ruling power left its mark on the city, contributing to a complex cultural heritage that blends Italian, French, and British influences.

Throughout its history, Valletta has also been a center of art and culture. It has hosted numerous artists, poets, and writers who have been inspired by its beauty and strategic location. Today, Valletta continues to celebrate this heritage with numerous museums, art galleries, and theaters, including the Manoel Theatre, one of the oldest working theaters in Europe. The city also hosts various cultural events and festivals that attract international artists and audiences, enhancing its reputation as a vibrant cultural hub.

Moreover, Valletta is not just about its past. The city has been actively engaged in preserving its cultural heritage while adapting to the needs of modern times. It was named a European Capital of Culture in 2018, a recognition that highlights its ongoing cultural vitality and its efforts in cultural preservation and innovation. In exploring Valletta, visitors are not merely walking through a museum of ancient history but engaging with a living city that continues to evolve while respecting its past. The fusion of its historical sites, cultural institutions, and vibrant public life makes Valletta a unique place where history and modernity coexist harmoniously. Whether wandering through its narrow streets, exploring its grand edifices, or enjoying its lively festivals, Valletta offers an educational and enriching experience that connects visitors with the heart and soul of Malta.

Must-Visit Sites: St. John's Co-Cathedral, Lascaris War Rooms, Upper & Lower Barrakka Gardens

St. John's Co-Cathedral, the Lascaris War Rooms, and the Upper & Lower Barrakka Gardens collectively epitomize the historical and cultural richness of Valletta, Malta. Situated in the heart of the capital, these landmarks not only showcase Malta's architectural grandeur but also provide a profound insight into the strategic roles played throughout its storied past.

St. John's Co-Cathedral, completed in 1577 as the conventual church for the Knights of St. John, stands as a monument to Baroque architecture. It is one of Europe's most opulently decorated churches, featuring intricately carved stone walls, painted vaulted ceilings, and gilded side altars. The cathedral also houses an impressive collection of art, including Caravaggio's famous painting, which resides in the Oratory. Visitors often take guided tours to fully appreciate the art and history of this magnificent cathedral, walking among nearly 400 tombstones of knights and officers that pave the cathedral floor.

Just a short walk away, nestled beneath the Upper Barrakka Gardens, are the Lascaris War Rooms. This network of underground tunnels and chambers served as the War Headquarters during the Second World War, directing the defense of Malta. The strategic significance of Malta during WWII is brought to life through detailed exhibits and wartime paraphernalia, offering visitors a comprehensive overview of the operations directed from these rooms.

Above these war rooms, the Upper & Lower Barrakka Gardens offer a peaceful retreat with panoramic views of the Grand Harbour and the Three Cities. These gardens are not only a place for relaxation and enjoyment of the lush greenery but also a vantage point for understanding Malta's strategic maritime importance. The daily firing of the noon-day gun is a tradition observed at the Upper Barrakka Gardens, attracting many to this ceremonial event. The gardens also feature various sculptures and monuments, such as the one dedicated to Sir Alexander Ball, which further enrich the historical landscape.

Each of these sites is easily accessible by public transport, with several buses stopping near the sites in Valletta. For those exploring on foot, the city's compact nature makes it easy to move between these historic sites, allowing for a seamless experience of stepping back in time. Whether it's understanding the profound history encapsulated within the walls of St. John's Co-Cathedral, exploring the strategic depths of the Lascaris War Rooms, or strolling through the tranquil Barrakka Gardens, visiting these landmarks provides a comprehensive and enriching exploration of Valletta's past and present.

Museums: National War Museum, National Archaeology Museum, Malta at War Museum

In Malta, the richness of the island's history is prominently displayed in its museums, each dedicated to different facets of its past. The National War Museum, the National Archaeology Museum, and the Malta at War Museum are key institutions that offer comprehensive insights into Malta's extensive historical and cultural heritage.

The National War Museum, located in Fort St. Elmo in Valletta, offers a compelling recount of Malta's role in military history, particularly during World War II. The museum houses an extensive collection of artifacts that are symbolic of Malta's courage during the sieges it has endured, including the George Cross awarded to the island by King George VI for bravery in the Second World War. Getting to the museum is straightforward; it is situated at the tip of the Valletta peninsula and is easily accessible by bus or a short walk from any location within the capital. Visitors can engage with interactive displays and view historical military equipment, making it an enriching experience for history buffs and families alike.

A short distance away, in the heart of Valletta, is the National Archaeology Museum, housed in the Auberge de Provence, a beautiful example of Baroque architecture. This museum offers a journey through Malta's prehistoric periods, featuring artifacts from the Neolithic through the Phoenician Period. Noteworthy are the famous figurines and sculptures from ancient temple sites, such as the Venus of Malta and the Sleeping Lady. Visitors to this museum will gain insights into the island's earliest inhabitants and their way of life, making it an essential visit for those interested in archaeology and ancient history. The museum's central location makes it easily reachable by public transportation or on foot, and nearby cafes and shops provide pleasant spots for relaxation after a museum tour.

On the other hand, the Malta at War Museum, located in Vittoriosa (Birgu), focuses specifically on Malta's experience during World War II. It is housed in a historic army barracks that served as an air raid shelter during the war, offering an authentic setting that enhances the visitor experience. The museum includes a well-preserved air raid shelter which visitors can explore, giving a real sense of the conditions experienced by the Maltese during the conflict. To get there, visitors can take a ferry from Valletta to the Three Cities and enjoy a scenic ride across the Grand Harbour, followed by a short walk to the museum.

Each museum not only showcases unique collections but also provides educational programs and guided tours that enrich the visitor experience. Engaging with the exhibits at these museums offers a deeper understanding of Malta's pivotal moments in history—from ancient civilizations through its heroic roles in wartime. Whether you are delving into ancient art at the Archaeology Museum, exploring wartime relics at the National War Museum, or walking through air raid shelters at the Malta at War Museum, these experiences promise to make your visit memorable and provide profound insights into the resilient spirit and rich history of Malta.

Gozo: The Island Sanctuary

Gozo, often referred to as the island sanctuary, is a smaller, more tranquil counterpart to the main island of Malta. Located just to the northwest of Malta, Gozo is known for its picturesque landscapes, serene atmosphere, and rich cultural heritage. This smaller island offers a distinct experience from the main island, with its rustic countryside, quiet towns, and stunning coastal views.

Getting to Gozo is straightforward. The most common way to reach the island is by ferry from Ċirkewwa on the northwestern tip of Malta to Mġarr on Gozo. The ferry service is frequent, operates daily, and the journey takes about 25 minutes. Upon arrival in Mġarr, visitors can explore the island by public buses, which are available right outside the ferry terminal, or by renting a car, which offers greater flexibility to explore the scenic routes at one's own pace.

Gozo is a haven for those seeking both relaxation and adventure. The island's landscape is dotted with historical sites, from the ancient Ġgantija Temples, which are among the oldest free-standing structures in the world, to the medieval Citadel in Victoria, the capital city of Gozo. These sites not only offer a glimpse into the island's past but also provide stunning views of the surrounding countryside and coast.

For outdoor enthusiasts, Gozo offers a plethora of activities. Hiking trails abound, with paths leading through lush valleys and along dramatic cliff tops offering expansive views of the Mediterranean. Diving is another popular activity, with Gozo boasting some of the best dive sites in the Mediterranean, including the famous Blue Hole and the recently created underwater dive park at Xatt l-Aħmar.

Beach lovers will find plenty of spots to relax, from the red sands of Ramla Bay, considered one of the best beaches on the island, to the more secluded bays of San Blas and Dwejra. Each location offers a unique seaside experience, from sunbathing and swimming to snorkeling and watching spectacular sunsets.

Cultural experiences in Gozo are deeply enriching, with the island's towns and villages hosting various festas (feasts) throughout the year. These festas are vibrant and colorful, celebrating patron saints with processions, fireworks, music, and food. Experiencing a Gozitan festa provides deep insight into the community spirit and religious devotion that characterize the island's culture.

Visitors should also not miss the opportunity to taste Gozitan cuisine, which is distinct from that of the main island. Local restaurants and farmhouses offer dishes made with fresh, locally sourced ingredients, including cheeselets made from sheep's milk, sun-ripened tomatoes, and freshly caught seafood.

Gozo is a place where time seems to slow down, inviting visitors to relax, explore, and immerse themselves in the natural beauty and historical wonders of the island. It's a sanctuary not just in terms of its serene landscapes and leisurely pace of life, but also as a haven for preserving the rich tapestry of cultural traditions that define this unique island in the Mediterranean.

Historical Sites: Ggantija Temples, The Old Prison

The Ggantija Temples and The Old Prison are two of Malta's most significant historical sites, each offering a unique window into the island's rich and varied past. Located on the island of Gozo, these sites provide not just insight into historical events, but also a deep connection to the cultural and societal norms of their respective eras.

The Ggantija Temples, situated in the village of Xaghra on Gozo, are renowned for being some of the oldest free-standing structures in the world, predating Stonehenge and the Egyptian pyramids. These megalithic temples were constructed during the Neolithic period, around 3600-3200 BC, making them over 5500 years old. The site consists of two temple structures, each featuring a series of elliptical chambers, or apses, built with large limestone slabs. The name 'Ggantija' derives from the Maltese word for 'giant,' as local legend holds that the temples were built by giants.

To visit Ggantija, tourists can take a direct bus from the Mgarr ferry terminal to Xaghra, or drive, which allows for greater flexibility in exploring the surrounding area. At the site, visitors can walk through the temple complex with the aid of informational plaques that explain the archaeological findings and hypotheses about the site's religious and ritualistic uses. The adjacent visitor center offers detailed exhibits on the Neolithic period in Malta, featuring artifacts discovered at the site and interactive displays that enhance the educational experience.

Just a short distance from the Ggantija Temples, in the heart of Victoria (Rabat), the capital city of Gozo, stands The Old Prison. Located adjacent to the Courts of Justice to which it was originally connected, the prison dates back to the mid-16th century, during the period of the Knights of St. John. The prison was used to incarcerate both common criminals and knights found guilty of various offenses until the second half of the 19th century.

Visitors to The Old Prison can explore the small complex that includes cells carved out of the rock, an exercise yard, and graffiti-covered walls that tell stories of former inmates. The graffiti, etched into the limestone, ranges from simple names and dates to elaborate carvings of ships, games, and intricate patterns, offering a poignant glimpse into the lives of those confined there. Tours often include insights into the types of crimes that led to imprisonment and the conditions within the prison, providing a stark contrast to the grandeur of other historical sites in Malta.

Both the Ggantija Temples and The Old Prison offer unique opportunities to delve into Malta's prehistoric religious practices and its later medieval penal system, respectively. For those looking to make the most of their visit, participating in a guided tour is highly recommended. These tours are usually led by knowledgeable guides who provide richer historical context and point out details that might otherwise be overlooked. Additionally, combining these visits with stops at nearby attractions, such as the Xaghra Stone Circle and the Ta' Kola Windmill, can make for a full day of historical exploration and learning, truly enhancing the visitor experience on the island of Gozo.

Natural Beauty: Ta' Cenc Cliffs, Ninu's Cave

Ta' Cenc Cliffs and Ninu's Cave are two of Gozo's natural treasures, each offering unique landscapes and fascinating geological features that highlight the island's natural beauty. These sites not only provide scenic views but also serve as gateways to understanding the natural history and ecological diversity of Malta.

Ta' Cenc Cliffs

Located on the southern coast of Gozo, the Ta' Cenc Cliffs are one of the island's most impressive natural landmarks. Rising sharply to heights of over 140 meters, these cliffs offer breathtaking views of the Mediterranean Sea and the surrounding landscape. The area is a haven for various species of flora and fauna, some of which are endemic to Malta, making it an important site for nature lovers and conservationists.

Getting to the Ta' Cenc Cliffs is relatively straightforward. Visitors can drive or take a bus to the nearby village of Sannat and then follow marked trails that lead to the cliffs. The walk itself is an invigorating experience, with well-trodden paths that meander through typical Mediterranean scrubland and limestone outcrops.

Activities at Ta' Cenc include bird watching, as the cliffs are a popular spot for migratory birds, and hiking along the cliff tops, which provide panoramic views of the sea and the opportunity to discover secluded coves along the coastline. The area is also of significant archaeological interest, with several ancient cart ruts and dolmens scattered around, adding a historical dimension to the visit.

Ninu's Cave

Ninu's Cave, located in the village of Xaghra, presents a different aspect of Gozo's natural beauty. It is an underground cave known for its impressive stalactites and stalagmites formations. Discovered in the late 19th century by local resident Joseph Rapa, the cave is a small but fascinating example of subterranean geology.

To visit Ninu's Cave, travelers can make their way to Xaghra either by public transport or by car. The cave is situated beneath a private house, making it one of the more unusual tourist sites. Visitors are typically given a guided tour by the owners, who explain the geological formations and the history of the cave's discovery.

Inside Ninu's Cave, the air is cool and damp, contrasting sharply with the often arid external environment of the island. The cave's formations are illuminated by artificial lighting, highlighting their intricate details and creating a surreal atmosphere that feels like stepping into another world.

Visiting Ninu's Cave provides not only a glimpse into the geological past of Malta but also an intimate experience that contrasts with the more expansive landscapes of Ta' Cenc Cliffs. The combination of these two sites offers a comprehensive view of Gozo's natural diversity, from the dramatic coastal cliffs to the quiet, hidden world beneath the island's surface.

Exploring both Ta' Cenc Cliffs and Ninu's Cave allows visitors to appreciate the variety of Gozo's natural attractions. Whether it's the vast, open views from the cliffs or the enclosed, whisper-quiet chambers of the cave, each experience enriches the understanding of Malta's unique natural heritage and provides memorable moments that are both educational and inspiring.

Cultural Museums: Gozo Archaeology Museum, Gozo Cathedral Museum

The Gozo Archaeology Museum and the Gozo Cathedral Museum are two cultural gems located in the heart of Victoria, the capital city of Gozo, Malta. These museums not only house significant historical and religious artifacts but also serve as gateways to understanding the rich cultural tapestry of Gozo and Malta at large.

Gozo Archaeology Museum

Situated in the oldest square of Victoria, the Gozo Archaeology Museum is housed in a beautiful 17th-century building that was once a townhouse. This museum offers a profound insight into the island's history, spanning from prehistoric times to the early modern period. Its collections include artifacts from the Ġgantija Temples, various Bronze Age sites, and Roman ruins that highlight the extensive historical narrative of human habitation on the island.

Visitors can reach the Gozo Archaeology Museum easily by public transport or car. The museum is located near the central bus station in Victoria, making it accessible for anyone exploring the city. For those driving, parking can be found in the vicinity of the city center.

The museum is organized chronologically, allowing visitors to walk through time, from Neolithic carved stones to Roman pottery and medieval architectural fragments. Each artifact is accompanied by detailed descriptions that enrich visitors' understanding of Gozo's archaeological heritage. The museum also offers guided tours which can be booked in advance, providing a more in-depth exploration of the exhibits.

Gozo Cathedral Museum

Just a short walk from the Gozo Archaeology Museum, the Gozo Cathedral Museum is another culturally significant site. Located within the citadel that dominates Victoria's skyline, this museum is part of the Gozo Cathedral complex. The museum showcases a range of ecclesiastical art, vestments, and sacred relics collected from the cathedral and other churches across the island.

Getting to the Gozo Cathedral Museum is as straightforward as visiting the Archaeology Museum, with both attractions being close to each other. Visitors often combine trips to both museums for a full cultural experience.

Inside the Gozo Cathedral Museum, guests can marvel at intricate liturgical items, including silverware used in religious ceremonies, paintings depicting biblical scenes, and manuscripts that reveal Gozo's religious practices through the ages. The highlight for many is the collection of tapestries and the cathedral's richly inlaid marble floor, which tells stories of the diocese and its bishops.

Both museums not only offer a peek into the historical and cultural life of Gozo but also provide a quiet, reflective space away from the bustling tourist spots. Spending time in these museums is highly recommended for those who appreciate history and art. Each visit allows for a deeper appreciation of the island's past, enhancing the overall experience of Gozo's cultural landscape.

Exploring these museums provides a comprehensive view of the archipelago's rich heritage, making any visit to Gozo a more memorable and enlightening experience. Whether you are a history enthusiast, an art lover, or simply curious about the past, these museums offer valuable insights into the cultural fabric of Gozo and its people.

CHAPTER 7

Hidden Gems

Malta, a small archipelago in the Mediterranean, is a treasure trove of hidden gems waiting to be explored by those eager to venture beyond the well-trodden tourist paths. This chapter will guide you through some of the lesser-known yet equally fascinating corners of Malta, where history, culture, and natural beauty converge to offer unique experiences away from the mainstream attractions.

Our journey into Malta's hidden gems begins with the ancient streets of Mdina and Rabat, where history echoes through the narrow, winding paths and baroque architecture. These cities are not just relics of the past but living museums offering a window into the island's medieval and early modern periods. Close by, you will discover cultural sites steeped in history such as St. Paul's

Catacombs, which provide an underground glimpse into early Christian Malta, and the Roman Villa, showcasing the domestic life of Malta's ancient Roman inhabitants.

The natural wonders of Malta offer their own hidden stories, with the Blue Lagoon providing a slice of paradise with its crystal-clear waters ideal for snorkeling and swimming. Comino's hiking trails invite more adventurous souls to explore the rugged landscapes and capture panoramic views that are simply breathtaking.

Furthermore, Malta's commitment to conservation can be seen in its wildlife and nature reserves, where the local flora and fauna thrive. These areas are essential for biodiversity and offer tranquil retreats for those looking to connect with nature and enjoy the peaceful side of the Maltese Islands.

This chapter will delve deeper into each of these aspects, offering tips on how to fully appreciate the quiet beauty and historical significance of Malta's lesser-known sites. Whether you are a history enthusiast, a nature lover, or a culture seeker, discovering these hidden gems will enrich your understanding of Malta and provide memories that are both profound and personal.

Walking Through History: Streets of Mdina and Rabat

Walking through the historic streets of Mdina and Rabat in Malta is like stepping back in time. These ancient cities are rich tapestries woven with layers of history, each street and building echoing stories from Malta's colorful past. Located in the northern region of Malta, Mdina, known as the "Silent City," and its neighboring town, Rabat, offer a unique blend of medieval and baroque architecture set against the backdrop of modern Maltese life.

Location and Access

Mdina, once the capital of Malta, sits atop a hill with commanding views of the island. Rabat lies just outside Mdina's old walls, forming a larger urban area steeped in history. Both are accessible by public transportation, with several buses running from major locations like Valletta and Sliema to Mdina. For those driving, parking is available outside Mdina's walls, as the city itself is largely pedestrianized.

Exploring Mdina and Rabat

Walking through Mdina's narrow alleys, visitors are greeted by an atmosphere of solemn tranquility that befits its nickname. The well-preserved fortifications and structures tell tales of nobility and knights who walked the same paths centuries ago. Key attractions include the Mdina Cathedral, with its impressive architecture and art collections, and the nearby Mdina Dungeons, which offer a glimpse into the less savory aspects of its history.

Just a stroll away, Rabat plays a complementary historical role. It is home to the famous St. Paul's Catacombs, an extensive underground Roman burial site that visitors can explore to learn about ancient burial practices. The catacombs also highlight the early Christian heritage that is an integral part of Maltese history.

Things to Do

Visitors can enhance their walking tour by visiting the various museums and cultural sites scattered throughout Mdina and Rabat. The Mdina Experience provides an engaging audio-visual presentation on the city's history, ideal for first-time visitors. For those interested in natural history, the National Museum of Natural History, located in an 18th-century palazzo in Mdina, offers exhibits on Maltese geology, flora, and fauna.

Dining in Mdina and Rabat is also a historical experience, with several restaurants and cafes offering traditional Maltese cuisine in ancient buildings. Enjoying a meal or a coffee in these old cities is a pleasure that combines both culinary and architectural heritage. For a memorable experience, time your visit to coincide with one of the many festivals or events that take place in Mdina and Rabat, such as medieval festivals and classical music concerts, which bring the ancient streets to life with the sounds and sights of their historical past.

Walking through Mdina and Rabat is not just a touristic activity; it is an immersive journey into the heart of Maltese history. Every corner of these ancient cities offers a story, a piece of art, or an architectural wonder that makes the experience deeply enriching. Whether you are exploring the silent, shadowy streets of Mdina or delving into the subterranean world of Rabat's catacombs, the experience is a profound reminder of the rich cultural tapestry that is Malta.

Cultural Sites: St. Paul's Catacombs, Roman Villa, Natural History Museum

St. Paul's Catacombs, the Roman Villa, and the Natural History Museum are significant cultural sites in Malta that offer deep insights into the island's diverse history and natural environment. Located in the town of Rabat, these sites are central to understanding both the ancient and ecological narratives of Malta.

St. Paul's Catacombs represent one of the most fascinating and extensive early Christian burial complexes in the Mediterranean. Situated on the outskirts of the old Roman capital Melite (today's Mdina), the catacombs are an intricate network of underground tombs and are a testament to Malta's early Christian heritage. They are thought to date back to the 4th century and were in use up until the 8th century. Visitors can explore the labyrinth of interconnected passageways and tombs which feature a variety of pagan and Christian wall paintings and inscriptions. The site is easily accessible from Mdina by foot, and just a short bus ride from other major towns, making it a convenient stop for anyone exploring the area.

The Roman Villa, also known as Domvs Romana, is located just outside the walls of Mdina, in what was once the heart of Roman Melite. The villa is famous for its well-preserved mosaics and the remnants of a wealthy Roman household. The villa's museum displays artifacts from the site, including Roman glassware, pottery, and statues that offer a glimpse into the daily life of the Romans on the island. The Roman Villa is particularly easy to visit due to its proximity to Mdina and Rabat, with several signs leading to the site and a nearby bus stop that services routes from Valletta and other major locales.

The Natural History Museum is housed in an 18th-century magisterial palace, situated within the serene confines of Mdina. The museum provides a comprehensive overview of Malta's natural history, including geology, mineralogy, paleontology, and biodiversity. The displays are both educational and engaging, showcasing the indigenous flora and fauna of the island, as well as specimens from around the world. The museum's location in Mdina, a major tourist draw, ensures it is easily accessible by public and private transport with ample signage directing visitors to its location.

Visiting these sites provides not only a journey into the past but also a chance to engage with Malta's cultural and natural landscape through well-curated exhibits and guided tours that enhance the understanding of the island's rich heritage. Each location offers unique insights, from the spiritual and burial practices at St. Paul's Catacombs to the luxurious domestic life of the Romans at the Villa, and the diverse ecosystems presented in the Natural History Museum.

To make the experience truly memorable, it is recommended to participate in the guided tours often available at these sites, which provide deeper insights and contextual background that might otherwise be missed. Additionally, many of these sites host special events, workshops, and temporary exhibitions that can provide a richer, more comprehensive experience. Exploring these cultural sites allows visitors to connect with Malta's historical narratives and natural wonders in a profound and personal way.

Exploring the Blue Lagoon

The Blue Lagoon, located on the tiny island of Comino between Malta and Gozo, is one of Malta's most idyllic natural attractions. Known for its vivid turquoise waters and breathtaking marine environment, the Blue Lagoon is a slice of paradise that attracts visitors from all over the world. Its crystal-clear waters and white sandy seabed create a natural swimming pool that is perfect for various water activities.

Getting to the Blue Lagoon involves a short ferry or boat trip. The easiest access is from Cirkewwa on Malta or Mgarr on Gozo, where regular boat services take visitors directly to Comino. During the summer months, these trips are frequent, and many operators offer additional tours around Comino and its neighboring islets. Some visitors opt for chartering private boats for a more personalized experience, allowing them the freedom to explore the lagoon and surrounding coves at their own pace.

Once at the Blue Lagoon, visitors can indulge in a variety of activities. Swimming and snorkeling are among the most popular, with the clear waters offering perfect conditions to explore the vibrant aquatic life close to the shore. The lagoon's sheltered position makes it ideal for families with children, who can play safely in the shallow waters. For the more adventurous, kayaking and paddleboarding provide unique ways to traverse the lagoon and discover secluded areas along Comino's rugged coastline.

Aside from water-based activities, the Blue Lagoon is also a fantastic spot for photography. The contrast of the bright blue waters against the rocky landscape provides stunning visuals at any time of the day. For those looking to relax, there are limited areas with sunbeds and umbrellas for rent, although arriving early to secure a spot is advisable due to the lagoon's popularity during peak season.

Visitors should be prepared for basic facilities on Comino, as the island is largely uninhabited. Carrying water, sun protection, and snacks is recommended. Despite its popularity, the Blue Lagoon retains its serene beauty, especially outside the peak hours of midday when the morning and late afternoon offer quieter moments to enjoy the picturesque setting.

Exploring the Blue Lagoon not only offers a day of spectacular natural beauty but also the chance to relax and unwind in one of Malta's most iconic landscapes. Whether snorkeling among the fishes, paddling through the azure waters, or simply soaking up the Mediterranean sun, a trip to the Blue Lagoon is a memorable part of any visit to Malta, offering both tranquility and the allure of an island paradise.

Comino's Hiking Trails and Viewpoints

Comino, the smallest of Malta's three inhabited islands, offers a tranquil escape with its network of hiking trails and scenic viewpoints. Known for its crystal-clear waters and the famous Blue Lagoon, Comino is also a haven for nature lovers and those seeking a peaceful retreat into natural landscapes.

Location and Access

Comino is located between the islands of Malta and Gozo. It can be reached by ferry services that operate from Cirkewwa on Malta and Mgarr on Gozo. These ferries typically drop visitors at the Blue Lagoon, but there are also options for water taxis and private boat charters that provide more flexibility and can take visitors closer to different starting points for hikes around the island.

Hiking Trails and Viewpoints

The hiking trails on Comino are relatively easy, making them accessible to hikers of all skill levels, and they offer some of the best ways to explore the island's natural beauty. One popular trail leads from the Blue Lagoon to Santa Marija Bay and on to the island's highest point. This trek not only offers panoramic views of Comino but also of Malta and Gozo in the distance. The paths wind through wild thyme and other endemic plants, providing a sensory experience of Comino's diverse flora.

Another significant trail leads to the St. Mary's Tower, an imposing watchtower built by the Knights of St. John in 1618. This historic structure offers an insight into Comino's role in the defense of the Maltese archipelago. The tower is often open to visitors, depending on the season, and from its upper reaches, one can enjoy sweeping views of both sister islands and the vast Mediterranean.

Activities and Things to Do

Apart from hiking, Comino is an excellent place for birdwatching, especially during the migration seasons when various bird species use the island as a resting point. The quiet and relatively undisturbed environment makes it ideal for nature photography, with spring and autumn providing lush colors and a variety of blooms.

Visitors can also explore the island's rugged coastline, where secluded bays and dramatic cliffs offer moments of solitude and spectacular sunset views. While the infrastructure on Comino is minimal, this lack of development is what preserves its charm and makes a day trip here a refreshing step back from the busier main islands.

Preparation and Considerations

When planning a trip to Comino, it's important to bring essentials such as water, snacks, and sun protection, as the amenities on the island are limited. Wearing comfortable walking shoes is advisable as the terrain, while not challenging, involves some rocky paths. It's also a good idea to check the weather forecast and ferry schedules in advance to ensure a smooth trip.

Exploring Comino's hiking trails and enjoying its stunning viewpoints provide a memorable experience that goes beyond the typical tourist spots. The island's mix of natural beauty, historical sites, and tranquility makes it a must-visit for anyone seeking to connect with nature and history in a serene setting. Whether you are trekking to a secluded viewpoint or watching the sunset from a quiet beach, Comino offers a peaceful escape into the heart of the Mediterranean's untouched landscapes.

Wildlife and Nature Reserves

Malta, with its unique Mediterranean climate and rich biodiversity, is home to several wildlife and nature reserves that offer a glimpse into the island's natural beauty and ecological importance. These reserves are crucial for the conservation of local flora and fauna, providing sanctuary to many species that are native to the region. Exploring these areas offers visitors a chance to connect with nature and learn about the delicate ecosystems that thrive in Malta.

One of the most significant nature reserves in Malta is the Ghadira Nature Reserve, located in Mellieha in the northern part of the island. This wetland reserve is a haven for birdwatchers, as it serves as a stopover for migratory birds traveling between Europe and Africa. The reserve covers an area of about 6 hectares and includes a variety of habitats, such as freshwater pools, reed beds, and salt marshes, all of which support a diverse range of bird species. Visitors can observe birds such as herons, flamingos, and various species of ducks from the well-placed bird hides around the reserve. The best time to visit Ghadira is during the spring and autumn migration seasons when the reserve is teeming with birdlife. The reserve is easily accessible by bus from Valletta or by car, with parking available nearby.

Another important site is the Is-Simar Nature Reserve, located in Xemxija, near St. Paul's Bay. Like Ghadira, Is-Simar is a wetland reserve that provides crucial habitat for birds and other wildlife. The reserve is managed by BirdLife Malta and features a visitor center that offers educational exhibits about the local ecosystem. The reserve's walking trails allow visitors to explore the area while observing the diverse bird species that inhabit the wetlands. Is-Simar is also an excellent place for photography, especially in the early morning or late afternoon when the light is perfect for capturing the beauty of the landscape and its inhabitants.

The Majjistral Nature and History Park, located in the northwest of Malta, is another must-visit for nature enthusiasts. Spanning over 6 kilometers of coastline, this park is Malta's first national park and covers a wide range of habitats, including garigue, rocky shores, and sandy beaches. The park is home to various plant species, many of which are endemic to the Maltese Islands. Visitors can explore the park on foot, following one of the many hiking trails that offer stunning views of the Mediterranean Sea and the surrounding countryside. The park is also rich in history, with several archaeological sites and remnants of World War II fortifications scattered throughout the area. To reach Majjistral Park, visitors can take a bus from Valletta to Mellieha or Golden Bay, and from there, it's a short walk to the park's entrance.

Another site of ecological importance is the Buskett Gardens, located near Rabat. While primarily known as a woodland area, Buskett is also a key habitat for various bird species, including the endangered Maltese falcon. The gardens, which were originally planted by the Knights of St. John as a hunting ground, now serve as a peaceful retreat for nature lovers and birdwatchers. The dense forest, made up of native and exotic trees, provides a cool and shaded environment, making it a perfect spot for a leisurely walk or a picnic. Buskett is particularly beautiful in the spring when wildflowers bloom, adding vibrant colors to the landscape. The gardens are easily accessible by bus or car, with ample parking available nearby.

Exploring these wildlife and nature reserves in Malta is not only a way to enjoy the island's natural beauty but also an opportunity to learn about the importance of conservation efforts in protecting these precious ecosystems. Whether you are birdwatching at Ghadira, hiking through Majjistral, or enjoying the tranquility of Buskett

Gardens, these reserves offer unforgettable experiences that deepen your appreciation for Malta's rich natural heritage. Each reserve provides educational resources, guided tours, and opportunities for photography, ensuring that visitors leave with a greater understanding of the delicate balance that sustains Malta's diverse wildlife and natural landscapes.

CHAPTER 8

Southern Malta: The Archaeological Region

Southern Malta, known as the Archaeological Region, is a captivating area that offers a unique glimpse into the island's ancient past intertwined with stunning natural landscapes. This part of Malta is not just a testament to the island's historical significance but also a showcase of its natural beauty, making it a must-visit for both history enthusiasts and nature lovers.

In this chapter, we will explore the renowned Hagar Qim and Mnajdra Temples, two of Malta's most extraordinary megalithic sites, which stand as a testament to the island's prehistoric inhabitants' architectural and astronomical prowess. These temples are set against the backdrop of the Mediterranean Sea, offering not only a historical journey but also breathtaking views that connect visitors with the land as it was thousands of years ago.

Further enhancing Southern Malta's appeal is the Blue Grotto, an astonishing natural wonder characterized by its deep blue waters and spectacular cave formations. A visit here often includes a boat tour, allowing you to experience the grotto's beauty from the water, capturing the shimmering reflections and vibrant colors that make this site a photographer's paradise.

Lastly, the chapter will take you along the scenic Mtahleb Cliffs, where rugged paths offer exhilarating coastal walks that reveal the raw beauty of Malta's coastline. The cliffs provide not just a chance for invigorating hikes but also moments of contemplation as you gaze out over the sea, where the sky meets the rocky shores.

Exploring Southern Malta is an experience that combines archaeological discovery with the joy of the outdoors, bringing to life the rich tapestry of Malta's cultural heritage and natural splendor. Whether you are tracing the steps of ancient civilizations through their temples or soaking in the sunlit beauty of the Mediterranean landscape, Southern Malta offers a deeply rewarding journey that resonates with the spirit of exploration and discovery.

Hagar Qim & Mnajdra Temples

The Hagar Qim and Mnajdra Temples, located on the southern coast of Malta, near the village of Qrendi, are among the most important archaeological sites on the island and represent a significant part of Malta's cultural heritage. These temples, built during the Neolithic period, around 3600-3200 BC, are remarkable for their age, architectural sophistication, and astronomical alignment, offering a fascinating glimpse into Malta's prehistoric past.

Location and Access

Hagar Qim and Mnajdra are situated approximately 2 kilometers apart from each other, perched on a hilltop overlooking the sea, providing not only a historical experience but also panoramic views of the Mediterranean. The easiest way to reach these temples is by car, with a well-signposted route from the main road leading directly to a large visitor center. Public transport options are also available, with buses running regularly from major towns, including Valletta and Mdina, to Qrendi, followed by a short walk to the site.

Exploring the Temples

Visiting Hagar Qim and Mnajdra allows you to walk through multi-room complexes made from gigantic limestone slabs, some of which weigh several tons. The layout of these temples, with their semicircular apses and central corridors, showcases the advanced building techniques and architectural skills of their builders. Informational signs and an audio-visual show at the visitor center provide insights into the life of the temple builders and the likely purposes of these structures, which include ritual and ceremonial functions.

The visitor center, which serves as the gateway to both temples, offers detailed models and exhibits that explain the significance of the temples' alignments with celestial bodies. The spring and autumn equinoxes illuminate the Mnajdra's main altar through a specially positioned doorway, demonstrating the builders' understanding of astronomy.

Things to Do

Apart from exploring the temples themselves, visitors can participate in guided tours that offer deeper insights into the history and archaeology of the sites. These tours often highlight the construction techniques, the purpose of various architectural features, and the artifacts found during excavations, including pottery, tools, and figurines.

Photography is another popular activity due to the picturesque setting of the temples against the backdrop of the blue sea and sky. The surrounding landscape, characterized by rocky outcrops and Mediterranean scrubland, is ideal for short hikes or leisurely walks, allowing visitors to appreciate the natural beauty of the area.

Making the Experience Memorable

To make the most of your visit, consider arriving early in the morning or late in the afternoon to avoid the crowds and to catch the best light for photography. The peaceful atmosphere during these times enhances the mystical feeling of the site and allows for a more personal connection with the ancient past. Additionally, attending special events or temporary exhibitions that are occasionally held at the visitor center can enrich your understanding of Malta's Neolithic heritage.

Visiting the Hagar Qim and Mnajdra Temples offers not only a journey back in time but also an opportunity to reflect on the ingenuity and spirituality of Malta's ancient inhabitants. It's a profound experience that connects visitors with the deep historical roots and breathtaking natural environment of this unique island.

Exploring the Blue Grotto

The Blue Grotto, located on the southern coast of Malta near the village of Wied iz-Zurrieq, is one of the island's natural marvels. Known for its shimmering blue waters and the stunning geological formations surrounding it, the Blue Grotto comprises several sea caverns, each offering its own unique view. This picturesque locale attracts visitors who come to marvel at the vibrant colors and the serene atmosphere.

Location and Access

The Blue Grotto is easily accessible from Valletta and other major towns in Malta. By car, it takes about 25 minutes from Valletta, following the signs to Wied iz-Zurrieq. There is a parking area close to the site from where you can easily walk to the viewing platforms or the boat embarkation points. Public buses also run regularly from Valletta and other towns to Wied iz-Zurrieq, making it convenient for those relying on public transport.

Boat Tours

One of the best ways to experience the Blue Grotto is by taking a boat tour. These tours are conducted in small traditional Maltese boats known as 'luzzus' and typically last around 20-30 minutes. The boatmen expertly navigate through the caves, including the renowned Honeymoon Cave and the Reflection Cave, where the phosphorescent colors of the underwater flora are mirrored on the cave walls due to the clear blue waters, creating a mesmerizing effect.

Photography and Sightseeing

The Blue Grotto is a haven for photographers, thanks to the play of light and the myriad of colors that change throughout the day. Morning, especially, is considered the best time to visit when the sunlight directly enters the caves, making the blue of the water appear even more luminous. The viewing platform on the mainland also offers spectacular views of the grotto and is a perfect spot for taking panoramic photos of the sea and the sky horizon.

Diving and Snorkeling

For the more adventurous, the Blue Grotto is also a popular diving and snorkeling spot. The clarity of the water provides excellent visibility, revealing a rich marine life that thrives beneath the surface. Various diving centers on the island offer guided diving tours to the Blue Grotto, catering to both beginners and experienced divers.

Local Cuisine

After exploring the caves, visitors can enjoy fresh seafood and traditional Maltese dishes at the nearby restaurants and kiosks. The local eateries offer a relaxed atmosphere where you can enjoy the local culinary delights while gazing out at the Mediterranean Sea.

Making the Most of Your Visit

To truly enjoy the Blue Grotto, it's advisable to visit during the off-peak seasons or early in the morning to avoid the crowds that can accumulate during the midday and peak tourist seasons. Engaging with the local boatmen and guides not only enriches the experience but also helps in understanding the geological and historical significance of the caves.

Visiting the Blue Grotto provides an unforgettable experience where natural beauty, adventure, and tranquility meet. Whether you are gliding through the majestic caves, capturing the scenic beauty through your lens, or simply soaking in the sun and the sea breeze, the Blue Grotto leaves an indelible mark on all who visit this natural wonder of Malta.

Coastal Walks at Mtahleb Cliffs

The Mtahleb Cliffs, located on the western coast of Malta, offer some of the most stunning and rugged landscapes on the island. These cliffs present a fantastic opportunity for those looking to explore Malta's natural beauty through coastal walks that combine breathtaking views, a serene environment, and the chance to observe local wildlife in its natural habitat.

Location and Access

Mtahleb Cliffs are situated near the small village of Mtahleb, which lies to the west of Rabat and Mdina. The area can be reached by car, with roads leading up to a point where visitors can park before proceeding on foot. For those using public transport, buses run from major cities like Valletta to Rabat, from where you can take a taxi to the cliffs, as the bus services do not extend directly to the cliffs.

Exploring the Cliffs

The coastal walks along the Mtahleb Cliffs are not just about exercise; they are an immersive experience into the natural and untouched side of Malta. The trails vary in difficulty, offering options for both serious hikers and those looking for a leisurely stroll. The paths along the cliff tops provide panoramic views of the open sea and the unspoiled Maltese countryside, making every step a picturesque moment.

As you walk along these cliffs, you will encounter a variety of flora and fauna, including endemic plants that are adapted to the Mediterranean climate. The area is also a popular spot for birdwatching, especially during migration seasons when birds such as shearwaters and falcons can be seen gliding over the cliffs.

Things to Do

Apart from walking and hiking, the Mtahleb Cliffs are a great place for photography enthusiasts. The natural scenery, especially at sunrise or sunset, creates a perfect backdrop for stunning photographs. The area is also conducive for picnics, with several spots along the trails where you can sit and enjoy a meal while taking in the views.

For those interested in history and culture, the vicinity of the cliffs is dotted with small chapels and ancient ruins that add a historical dimension to the walks. Exploring these sites provides a deeper understanding of Malta's rich heritage and the relationship between its people and the landscape.

Making the Experience Memorable

To make the most of your visit to the Mtahleb Cliffs, it's advisable to wear comfortable walking shoes and bring along sun protection, water, and snacks. The natural terrain can be challenging, so being well-prepared ensures that you can enjoy the walk without discomfort. Additionally, visiting during the cooler parts of the day, such as early morning or late afternoon, can make the walk more pleasant and allow you to avoid the midday heat.

Visiting the Mtahleb Cliffs offers a memorable experience for anyone looking to connect with nature, enjoy peaceful landscapes, and escape the more crowded tourist spots in Malta. It's an excursion that appeals to hikers, nature lovers, and anyone in search of tranquility and natural beauty. Whether you're tracing the coastline, spotting wildlife, or just enjoying the open air, the Mtahleb Cliffs provide a refreshing and rejuvenating outdoor adventure.

CHAPTER 9

Northern Malta: Coastal Adventures

Northern Malta, a region characterized by its vibrant coastal towns, diverse attractions, and natural beauty, offers a perfect setting for adventurers and families alike. This chapter delves into the unique coastal adventures that can be enjoyed in this lively part of the island, highlighting the seamless blend of entertainment, history, and nature.

We begin our journey in Mellieha, a town renowned for its picturesque beaches and the iconic Popeye Village. Originally built as a film set, Popeye Village has transformed into a charming family-friendly attraction, complete with colorful wooden buildings, boat rides, and themed entertainment that captivates visitors of all ages. Mellieha's beaches, known for their crystal-clear waters and extensive sand stretches, offer relaxation and a variety of water sports activities.

Moving to St. Paul's Bay, we explore its dual charm of historical significance and modern attractions. The National Aquarium is a focal point here, providing insights into Mediterranean marine life through meticulously designed habitats and interactive experiences. The bay area, with its serene coastal walks, invites visitors to unwind and enjoy the scenic views, encapsulating the essence of Malta's coastal allure.

Additionally, Salina National Park offers a nature retreat where birdwatching and scenic trails make it a haven for nature enthusiasts. The park's salt pans, an important part of Malta's historical salt production, now serve as a key site for bird migration, creating a unique eco-tourism experience.

Each of these locations in Northern Malta tells its own story, contributing to the rich tapestry of experiences that make the region a must-visit. From cinematic history to natural escapades and aquatic discoveries, Northern Malta presents a diverse palette of activities that promise memorable adventures for every traveler. Whether you're exploring the depths of the sea, relishing the tranquility of nature, or stepping into a fantasy village, this chapter will guide you through the best coastal adventures Northern Malta has to offer.

Mellieha: Popeye Village and Beaches

Mellieha, located on the northern coast of Malta, is celebrated for its picturesque landscapes, captivating beaches, and the charming Popeye Village. This area combines natural beauty with unique entertainment, making it a prime destination for visitors seeking both relaxation and fun activities in a scenic setting.

Popeye Village

Originally constructed as the film set for the 1980 musical production "Popeye," starring Robin Williams, Popeye Village has since been transformed into one of Malta's most beloved tourist attractions. Nestled in the beautiful bay of Anchor Bay, just a couple of kilometers west of Mellieha town center, this colorful village offers a playful escape into the world of Popeye the Sailor Man. The site is accessible by car, with ample parking available, or by public bus services that frequently run from major locations including

Valletta and Sliema, stopping near the entrance of the village.

Visitors to Popeye Village can explore the quaint wooden buildings, each intricately designed and painted to match the whimsical style of the movie. The village operates as a theme park where guests can enjoy various entertainment options including live shows, puppet performances, and cinema screenings that recount the making of the film. For families, there are playful activities and games, boat rides, and water trampolines, ensuring that children are as entertained as their parents.

Beaches in Mellieha

Mellieha is also famous for its beaches, which are among the best in Malta. The most renowned is Mellieha Bay, also known as Ghadira Bay, the largest sandy beach on the island. The beach is easily accessible by public transport or car, and there is a large parking area nearby. With shallow waters that gradually deepen, it is ideal for families with young children. The beach offers various facilities including sunbeds, umbrellas, beach bars, and water sports centers where visitors can rent equipment for windsurfing, kitesurfing, kayaking, and paddleboarding.

Another notable spot is Paradise Bay, located near the Cirkewwa ferry terminal, which provides services to the neighboring island of Gozo. This smaller, more secluded beach is known for its crystal-clear waters and is a favored spot for snorkeling and diving due to the abundant marine life and interesting underwater landscapes.

Making the Experience Memorable

To make the most of your visit to Mellieha, consider timing your activities to avoid the peak hours, especially if you're heading to the beaches. Early morning or late afternoon visits ensure fewer crowds and cooler temperatures, perfect for hiking or exploring the areas around the beaches, such as the nearby nature trails and historical sites. Additionally, sunset views from either Popeye Village or any of Mellieha's beaches offer breathtaking scenes that are perfect for memorable photographs.

Visiting Mellieha provides a delightful blend of adventure, history, and relaxation, all set against the backdrop of Malta's stunning natural beauty. Whether you're stepping into the quirky world of a film set or soaking up the sun on a sandy beach, Mellieha offers a comprehensive experience that caters to all ages and interests.

St. Paul's Bay: National Aquarium and Coastal Charm

St. Paul's Bay, located on the northeastern coast of Malta, is a popular destination known for its rich history, vibrant marine life, and beautiful coastal landscapes. Among its many attractions, the National Aquarium stands out as a must-visit for families, nature lovers, and anyone interested in marine conservation.

Qawra Seaside Leisure

Qawra, situated on the northern coast of Malta within the Saint Paul's Bay locality, offers a perfect blend of relaxation, entertainment, and scenic beauty, making it a favored destination for tourists and locals alike. This seaside resort is easily accessible by public transport, with frequent bus services from major cities like Valletta and Sliema, and by car, it is merely a 30-minute drive from the capital.

Upon arriving in Qawra, visitors are greeted with a stunning promenade stretching along the rocky coastline, ideal for leisurely walks with views of the open sea and the smaller islands of St. Paul's Bay. The promenade is lined with a variety of cafes and restaurants where one can savor fresh seafood and traditional Maltese cuisine while enjoying the Mediterranean breeze.

National Aquarium

The Malta National Aquarium is prominently situated in Qawra, part of the St. Paul's Bay area. This modern facility is easily accessible via the main road that runs along the northern coast of Malta. Visitors can reach the aquarium by car, with ample parking available on-site, or by using the public bus services that connect the aquarium to major localities, including Valletta and Sliema.

The aquarium's design is inspired by a starfish, reflecting its commitment to marine life and the environment. It houses over 175 species in 41 tanks, mirroring different marine and terrestrial habitats around the Maltese Islands and the Mediterranean Sea. From the grand main tank, filled with sharks, rays, and other large fish, to thematic tanks that represent Maltese historical episodes under the sea, the aquarium offers an immersive experience into the underwater world.

Visitors can participate in guided tours, feeding sessions, and interactive activities designed to educate about marine conservation and the ecology of the Mediterranean. The facility also includes a research center focusing on local marine studies and conservation initiatives, contributing to the preservation of marine biodiversity.

Coastal Charm of St. Paul's Bay

St. Paul's Bay itself is steeped in history, purportedly the location where Saint Paul was shipwrecked in 60 A.D. This historical context adds a rich cultural layer to the area, with several sites, including the iconic St. Paul's Shipwreck Church, enhancing the visitor experience. The bay area is perfect for leisurely strolls along the promenade where one can enjoy the bustling atmosphere, local eateries, and stunning sea views.

Outdoor activities abound in St. Paul's Bay, from leisurely walks along the rugged coastline to more adventurous water sports such as diving and snorkeling. The clear waters and the diversity of marine life make it a popular spot for divers looking to explore underwater caves and wrecks.

Making the Experience Memorable

To make your visit to St. Paul's Bay and the National Aquarium as enjoyable as possible, it is advisable to plan your activities early in the day to avoid the peak tourist hours, especially during the summer months. Morning visits not only allow for a more relaxed experience but also take advantage of the cooler temperatures for outdoor activities.

Enjoying a meal at one of the local seafront restaurants offers a taste of the region's culinary delights, with fresh seafood and traditional Maltese dishes enhancing the coastal experience. For those interested in cultural activities, checking local listings for festivals or events that coincide with your visit can provide a deeper insight into the community and its traditions.

St. Paul's Bay, with its blend of historical sites, modern attractions like the National Aquarium, and natural beauty, offers a comprehensive travel experience. Whether you are exploring the depths of the sea through interactive aquarium exhibits or soaking up the Mediterranean sun along the bay, St. Paul's Bay embodies a unique mix of education, history, and leisure activities suitable for all ages.

Birdwatching and Nature Trails at Salina National Park

Salina National Park, situated on the northeastern coast of Malta, near the towns of Naxxar and St. Paul's Bay, offers a unique blend of natural beauty, historical significance, and biodiversity. This protected area is known for its salt pans, which have been used for salt production since Roman times, and today, it serves as an important ecological site for birdwatching and nature walks.

Location and Access

Salina National Park is accessible by various means of transportation. For those driving, there is a designated parking area near the entrance of the park. Public buses from major cities like Valletta, Sliema, and Bugibba stop nearby, making it easy for tourists and locals alike to visit without personal vehicles. The park is equipped with walkways and signs, making navigation straightforward for all visitors.

Birdwatching

Salina is a haven for birdwatchers, especially during the migration seasons in spring and autumn when various bird species stop at the salt pans to rest and feed. The park's strategic location along bird migration routes across the Mediterranean makes it an ideal spot for observing a diverse range of migratory birds, including flamingos, herons, and various wading birds. Birdwatching enthusiasts can find several strategically placed hides throughout the park, offering unobtrusive views of the birds without disturbing them.

Nature Trails

The network of nature trails in Salina National Park provides visitors with the opportunity to explore the diverse habitats found within the park, from coastal shrublands to remnants of maquis. These trails are well-maintained and provide information boards that explain the flora and fauna of the area, as well as the ecological importance of salt pans and their role in supporting biodiversity.

Activities and Conservation

Apart from birdwatching and walking, Salina National Park offers educational tours and workshops that focus on environmental conservation and the history of salt production in Malta. These programs are designed to engage visitors of all ages, providing valuable insights into the efforts made to preserve and enhance the park's natural and historical landscapes.

Making the Experience Memorable

To make the most out of your visit to Salina National Park, it is advisable to bring binoculars for birdwatching, comfortable walking shoes, and adequate sun protection, as the area can be quite exposed. Early morning or late afternoon visits are recommended, as the birds are most active during these times, and the lighting is ideal for photography. For those interested in a deeper understanding of the area's ecology and history, participating in a guided tour can enrich the experience.

Visiting Salina National Park is not only a chance to enjoy Malta's natural beauty but also an opportunity to learn about the traditional crafts of salt harvesting and the modern conservation techniques used to maintain this delicate ecosystem. Whether you're an avid birdwatcher, a nature lover, or just looking for a peaceful place to unwind, Salina National Park offers a serene and educational escape into one of Malta's most cherished landscapes.

CHAPTER 10

Central Malta : Activities

Central Malta, nestled at the heart of the island, offers a vibrant tapestry of history and modernity, making it a compelling destination for tourists seeking a diverse range of activities. This chapter will guide you through some of the most intriguing attractions Central Malta has to offer, each providing a unique insight into the island's rich cultural heritage and its ongoing celebration of past and present.

We start with the Malta Aviation Museum, a fascinating venue located in Ta' Qali, once an airfield and now a site that captures the heroics of World War II aviation history. The museum boasts a remarkable collection of aircraft, engines, and aviation memorabilia that bring to life the significant role Malta played during the aerial battles of the 1940s. Here, history enthusiasts and families alike can explore exhibits that are both educational and engaging, offering a detailed look at the evolution of military and civilian aviation in Malta.

Another iconic site featured in this chapter is the Mosta Dome, renowned for being one of the largest unsupported church domes in the world. Located in the town of Mosta, this architectural marvel is not only a place of worship but also a symbol of resilience and hope, famously surviving a bomb drop during World War II without it detonating. Visitors can marvel at the exquisite interior and the awe-inspiring dome, with its detailed frescoes and ornate decorations, which provide a profound sense of the artistic achievements and spiritual depth of Malta.

Adding to the central delights, Qormi presents a deep dive into Malta's culinary tradition with its renowned bread-making and local festivities. Known as the hub for Malta's bread enthusiasts,

Qormi celebrates its legacy through annual festivals such as the Qormi Bread Festival, which not only honors the traditional Maltese bread but also showcases local arts, music, and culture. Visitors can experience the warmth of Qormi's community through interactive baking sessions and street celebrations that highlight the town's rich history and culinary expertise.

This chapter promises to provide a comprehensive overview of Central Malta's must-visit sites, blending historical significance with captivating narratives. Whether you're delving into the heroic tales of wartime pilots, gazing up at the majestic Mosta Dome, or indulging in the rich flavors of Qormi's bread-making traditions, Central Malta offers a journey through time that both educates and inspires. Each visit promises to enrich your understanding of Malta's multifaceted history, leaving you with lasting memories of the island's central treasures.

Aviation Museum

The Malta Aviation Museum, located in Ta' Qali, a former WWII airfield that is centrally positioned between Mdina and Mosta, offers an enthralling journey into the rich history of aviation on the island. The museum is a tribute to Malta's pivotal role in World War II and its aviation heritage that spans several decades.

Location and Access

The museum is easily accessible by car with signage from major roads leading directly to it. For those relying on public transport, buses from Valletta, Sliema, and other major locations run regularly to Ta' Qali. The nearest bus stop is just a short walk from the museum, making it convenient for visitors without personal vehicles.

Exploring the Malta Aviation Museum

Upon entering the museum, visitors are greeted with an extensive collection of aircraft, ranging from World War II fighters to post-war jets, including notable models like the Hawker Hurricane, Supermarine Spitfire, and the De Havilland Vampire. Each aircraft is meticulously restored, many of which are in airworthy condition, providing a real sense of history coming to life.

The museum also features a variety of exhibits that display aviation artifacts, uniforms, equipment, and engines. Each piece is accompanied by informative descriptions that explain their use and significance, offering insights into the technological advancements and the personal stories of those who served on the island.

Activities and Interactive Experiences

One of the highlights of the museum is the opportunity to participate in guided tours led by knowledgeable volunteers, many of whom are veterans with personal stories of Malta's aviation history. These tours enrich the visit, adding a personal touch that connects visitors with the past in a meaningful way.

For enthusiasts wanting a deeper dive, the museum offers hands-on workshops on aircraft restoration and preservation techniques. These sessions provide a unique behind-the-scenes look at the care and expertise required to maintain historical aircraft.

Making the Experience Memorable

The museum is not only about aircraft; it's also home to a well-stocked souvenir shop where visitors can purchase models, books, posters, and other memorabilia related to aviation. For families, the museum provides educational booklets and scavenger hunts to engage children and help them learn about aviation history in an interactive way.

Visiting the Malta Aviation Museum is more than a day out; it's an educational journey that offers a profound understanding of Malta's strategic importance in aviation history and its ongoing commitment to preserving this legacy. Whether you're an aviation enthusiast, a history buff, or looking for a unique educational outing, the Malta Aviation Museum provides a captivating experience that is both informative and memorable.

Mosta Dome: Marvel at One of the World's Largest Church Domes

The Mosta Dome, officially known as the Rotunda of Mosta, is an architectural marvel located in the heart of Mosta, a bustling town in central Malta. Renowned for having one of the largest unsupported domes in the world, this monumental structure is not only a significant place of worship but also a symbol of survival and resilience, making it a must-visit for anyone traveling to Malta.

Location and Access

Mosta Dome is centrally situated, making it easily accessible from various parts of the island. Visitors can reach Mosta by car via the main roads that connect it to neighboring towns and villages. There is parking available in the town center, though it can be limited during peak hours. Public transport is another convenient option, with several bus routes from Valletta, Sliema, and other major areas stopping near the church. The Mosta

Dome is prominently located in the town square, making it hard to miss.

Exploring the Mosta Dome

Upon entering the Mosta Dome, visitors are immediately struck by the massive scale of the interior. The dome, with a diameter of 37.2 meters, towers overhead, adorned with intricate frescoes and gold accents that illustrate biblical scenes. The design was inspired by Rome's Pantheon and was completed in the 19th century, a testament to the skill and ambition of its builder, Giorgio Grognet de Vassé, a local architect.

One of the most compelling aspects of the Mosta Dome is its history during World War II, when a bomb pierced the dome during an air raid but miraculously failed to explode. This event is commemorated by a replica of the bomb displayed inside the church, and the story is detailed on informational plaques, giving visitors insight into the miraculous event that has since become a part of local lore.

Activities and Things to Do
Visitors to the Mosta Dome can participate in guided tours that delve deeper into the history and architecture of the building. These tours often include access to parts of the church not usually open to the public, such as the roof, from where one can enjoy panoramic views of Mosta and beyond.

Photography enthusiasts will find plenty of opportunities to capture the stunning architecture from both inside and outside. The area around the church is also worth exploring, with several cafes and shops where you can enjoy a coffee or buy local crafts.

For those interested in religious art, the church houses an impressive collection of artworks, including statues and paintings donated by the local community over the years. The artistic details and the spiritual atmosphere provide a profound sense of peace and reflection.

Making the Experience Memorable

To fully appreciate the beauty and tranquility of the Mosta Dome, it is advisable to visit during less busy times, such as weekday mornings. Attending a mass, if possible, can also provide a deeper connection to the local community and the spiritual significance of the church.

Visiting the Mosta Dome offers a glimpse into the rich cultural and religious heritage of Malta. Its stunning architecture and the incredible story of survival during the war make it a fascinating destination for history buffs, architecture enthusiasts, and casual tourists alike. This iconic structure is not just a site of architectural grandeur but also a beacon of hope and faith for the Maltese people.

Qormi: Bread-Making and Local Festivities

Qormi, situated in the central part of Malta, is a town famous for its rich bread-making heritage and vibrant local festivities. Known historically as the hub of Malta's baking industry, Qormi's bakeries are renowned for producing traditional Maltese bread, which is a staple in the local diet.

Getting There
Qormi is easily accessible from Malta's capital, Valletta, and other major towns. Public buses regularly service the area, providing affordable and convenient transport options. For those preferring to drive, Qormi is well-connected by major roads, making it a short drive from most parts of the island.

Things to Do in Qormi
Bread-Making Experience: Visitors can immerse themselves in the bread-making process at one of the many traditional bakeries. Some

bakeries offer tours that allow you to witness the bread-making process from start to finish, and even participate in the baking.

Local Festivities: Qormi is particularly lively during the festa season. The town celebrates two major feasts, one dedicated to Saint George and the other to Saint Sebastian. These feasts are marked by elaborate decorations, fireworks, music, and processions, providing a deep dive into the local culture and community spirit.

Culinary Tours: Given its reputation for culinary delights, a guided food tour around Qormi can be a fulfilling experience. These tours not only focus on bread but also include other local foods and wines, offering a comprehensive taste of Maltese cuisine.

Cultural Sights: Explore the town's churches, such as the Church of St. George, which is an architectural marvel. The area also hosts several chapels and historical sites that reflect its past.

Memorable Experiences

Participate in a Bread-Making Workshop: Engage more deeply by taking part in a bread-making workshop where you can learn the traditional methods that have been passed down through generations.

Attend a Local Festa: Plan your visit during one of the festas for a truly unique and vibrant experience. The energy and joy during these festivals are contagious and offer wonderful photo opportunities and the chance to interact with locals.

Explore on Foot: Walking around Qormi, you can appreciate its charming architecture and stop by small local eateries and cafes where you can try traditional snacks and drinks.

Qormi offers a unique blend of culinary heritage and local traditions, making it a fascinating destination for those looking to experience the authentic lifestyle of Malta. Whether you're a food lover or a culture enthusiast, Qormi provides a memorable journey into the heart of Maltese community life.

CHAPTER 11

Western Malta: Landscapes and History

Western Malta, with its dramatic landscapes and rich historical tapestry, offers a distinctively serene and poignant experience for travelers. This chapter unveils the unique allure of the region, highlighting its profound military history, breathtaking natural beauty, and well-preserved gardens that together provide a comprehensive view of Malta's diverse heritage.

We start in Mtarfa, a town with a robust military legacy, characterized by its old British colonial buildings and the remnants of military infrastructure. The town's position on a plateau offers not just historical insights but also stunning views across the island, making it a fascinating stop for those interested in Malta's strategic importance in the past.

Next, the iconic Dingli Cliffs present one of Malta's most spectacular natural sights. These cliffs offer unobstructed views of the Mediterranean Sea, especially captivating at sunset when the sky and sea blend in a canvas of fiery colors. The cliffs are also a starting point for several nature trails that meander through the rugged terrain, providing opportunities for both leisurely walks and more challenging hikes.

Lastly, San Anton Gardens, located in the village of Attard, is one of the most beautiful and tranquil places in Western Malta. Originally part of a 17th-century villa, these gardens are meticulously maintained, displaying a wide variety of plants and flowers, alongside fountains and pathways that invite visitors to linger and enjoy the peaceful ambiance.

Each of these destinations in Western Malta offers its own unique experience, from the silent, historic streets of Mtarfa to the majestic, natural vistas at Dingli Cliffs and the lush, serene layouts of San Anton Gardens. Together, they encapsulate the essence of Western Malta—a region where history and nature exist in harmony, waiting to be explored by those eager to delve deeper into the island's captivating story.

Mtarfa: Military History and Natural Sights

Mtarfa, a small town in the northern region of Malta, is steeped in military history and surrounded by natural beauty. This area, once a significant base for the British Royal Navy and later the Royal Air Force, today stands as a serene locality that offers visitors a unique glimpse into Malta's strategic military past coupled with remarkable natural sights.

Location and Access

Mtarfa is situated on a high plateau overlooking the ancient city of Mdina and is adjacent to Rabat. It is easily accessible by car, and ample parking is available near major sites and residential areas. Public transport services are reliable, with several bus routes from Valletta and other major Maltese towns stopping in Mtarfa, making it convenient for tourists to reach this historically rich area.

Exploring Mtarfa's Military History

The town's military significance is evident in its architecture and the remnants of its military past. Visitors can explore the old military barracks, which have been partly converted into residential units while retaining much of their original character. The Mtarfa Military Cemetery is a poignant reminder of the town's history, containing graves of British servicemen and their families along with memorials from both world wars.

Natural Sights and Activities

Mtarfa's natural environment offers more than just a historical tour. The town provides panoramic views of the island, especially stunning at sunset. For nature enthusiasts, several walking trails lead from the town center into the surrounding countryside, offering opportunities to observe local flora and fauna in their natural habitat. These trails are suitable for all ages and provide a peaceful retreat from the more tourist-heavy areas of Malta.

Things to Do

One of the main attractions in Mtarfa is the Clock Tower, a well-preserved structure dating back to the British era, which is not only a historical monument but also provides a scenic vantage point for photographers and sightseers. Additionally, the nearby Royal Naval Hospital, although no longer in operation, is an impressive building that can be admired from the outside.

Visitors can also engage with the community through local events and festivals, often held in the main square, which celebrate both the town's history and its current cultural vibrancy. These events are a great way to experience local life and cuisine.

Making the Experience Memorable

To fully appreciate what Mtarfa has to offer, consider visiting during one of the local festivals, which often include guided tours of historical sites, exhibitions, and tastings of traditional Maltese food. Taking a leisurely walk through the town to appreciate its architecture and stopping at local eateries for a snack or meal can also enhance the visit.

Mtarfa offers a quiet, less commercialized experience of Malta, perfect for those interested in history and nature. Its blend of military heritage and natural beauty provides a unique backdrop for a memorable visit, making it a worthwhile destination for those looking to explore beyond the typical tourist paths.

Dingli Cliffs: Sunset Views and Nature Walks

Dingli Cliffs, located on the western coast of Malta, offer some of the most breathtaking views and tranquil nature walks on the island. Standing approximately 250 meters above sea level, these cliffs present a majestic natural frontier to the Mediterranean Sea, making them a favorite spot for both locals and tourists seeking a serene escape into nature.

Location and Access

Dingli Cliffs are easily accessible from the village of Dingli, a short drive from Rabat and other central locations in Malta. Visitors can reach the cliffs by car, with parking available along the roadside near the main viewing areas. Public transport is also an option, with buses running from major cities to Dingli village. From there, it's a pleasant walk or a short taxi ride to the cliffs.

Exploring Dingli Cliffs

The cliffs offer extensive walking trails that meander along the coastline, providing stunning vistas of the open sea and the tiny uninhabited island of Filfla. These trails are well-maintained, making them suitable for walkers of all abilities. The area is particularly renowned for its spectacular sunsets, where the sky and sea are painted with hues of orange, pink, and red, offering a perfect backdrop for photographers and romantic strolls alike.

Activities and Things to Do

One of the most popular activities at Dingli Cliffs is birdwatching, as the cliffs serve as a natural habitat for various bird species, especially during migration periods. The spring and autumn months are particularly rewarding for bird enthusiasts looking to spot rare migratory birds passing over Malta.

For those interested in history, a small detour from the main path leads to St. Mary Magdalene Chapel, an iconic landmark perched on the edge of the cliffs. This small chapel dates back to the 17th century and is often highlighted by its stark, picturesque presence against the landscape.

Making the Experience Memorable

To make the most of your visit to Dingli Cliffs, consider packing a picnic to enjoy along one of the scenic overlooks, where you can relax and soak in the Mediterranean sun. Wearing comfortable walking shoes is recommended, as exploring the trails can take a few hours, especially if you venture along the various paths that offer different perspectives of the sea and surrounding countryside.

Nature lovers might also appreciate a guided nature walk, which can be arranged through local tour operators who specialize in ecological and heritage tours. These guides provide insights into the flora and fauna of the area as well as the geological and historical significance of the cliffs.

Visiting Dingli Cliffs provides a peaceful yet invigorating experience, ideal for those looking to connect with nature and enjoy some of the most majestic views Malta has to offer. Whether you're there to witness the stunning sunset, enjoy a leisurely hike, or simply to find a quiet spot to reflect and unwind, Dingli Cliffs will not disappoint.

Exploring San Anton Gardens

San Anton Gardens, nestled in the heart of Attard, are among Malta's most beautiful and historically significant public gardens. Originally part of a private estate belonging to the Grand Masters of the Order of St. John, today these gardens are open to the public, offering a tranquil escape filled with lush greenery, ornate fountains, and a rich variety of flora.

Location and Access

San Anton Gardens are located in Attard, in central Malta, making them easily accessible from any part of the island. Visitors can drive to the gardens, with parking available in the vicinity. Public transport is also convenient; several bus routes serve the area, with stops nearby, ensuring that the gardens are reachable for those preferring not to drive.

Exploring San Anton Gardens

Upon entering San Anton Gardens, visitors are greeted by well-manicured walkways lined with ancient trees, some of which are over three centuries old. The gardens are renowned for their diverse plant species, ranging from local Mediterranean flora to exotic plants brought to Malta over the centuries. The layout of the gardens includes a main pathway that leads through various sections, each offering its own unique landscape and thematic focus.

Activities and Things to Do

One of the main attractions within the gardens is the ornamental ponds and fountains, which are home to ducks and swans. These features, along with the classical sculptures and busts that dot the landscape, create a picturesque environment ideal for photography enthusiasts and nature lovers.

The gardens also host a range of seasonal floral displays, which change throughout the year, providing a fresh experience with every visit. For those interested in botany or gardening, many of the plants are labeled with botanical names and origins, offering an educational component to the visit.

Making the Experience Memorable

Visitors can enhance their experience at San Anton Gardens by joining one of the guided tours available, which provide insights into the history of the gardens and the architectural features within them. These tours are especially popular during cultural events and festivals, when the gardens often host concerts, art exhibitions, and other public events.

For families, the gardens are equipped with various amenities, including picnic areas and small play spaces for children, making it a family-friendly destination where visitors can spend an entire afternoon relaxing and exploring.

Additional Tips

To fully enjoy the lush surroundings, visitors are advised to wear comfortable walking shoes and bring along a camera to capture the scenic beauty of the gardens. Additionally, checking the local event calendar before visiting can provide opportunities to coincide your visit with special activities and exhibitions.

San Anton Gardens not only offer a peaceful retreat from the urban hustle but also a glimpse into Malta's rich historical tapestry, making them a must-visit for anyone seeking a blend of natural beauty and cultural heritage. Whether you are a local resident or a tourist, a visit to these enchanting gardens promises a delightful and enriching experience.

CHAPTER 12

Entertainment and Nightlife

Malta transforms as the sun sets, revealing a vibrant entertainment and nightlife scene that caters to all tastes. From the bustling nightclubs of Paceville to the serene evenings spent at sea-view bars, this chapter will guide you through the diverse after-dark experiences that Malta offers. Whether you're looking to dance the night away in a club, enjoy a live band while sipping on local wines, or try your luck in a casino, Malta has an array of options to make every night memorable.

Paceville remains the beating heart of Malta's nightlife, renowned for its dynamic array of bars, clubs, and restaurants that cater to both the young and the young at heart. As we delve deeper, we'll explore other nightlife hubs scattered across the island, offering everything from chic rooftop lounges to laid-back beachfront establishments.

For those seeking entertainment beyond the conventional bar and club scene, Malta's Mediterraneo Marine Park and Splash & Fun Water Park offer thrilling daytime activities that transition into unique nighttime experiences during the summer months. Additionally, Malta is host to a vibrant festival calendar that celebrates everything from music and art to food and history, providing endless entertainment options throughout the year.

This chapter will not only highlight where to go and what to do but also offer practical tips on enjoying Malta's nightlife safely and to its fullest. Whether you are a solo traveler or with a group, looking for a wild night out or a taste of local culture, you'll find that Malta's nights are as enriching as they are exciting.

Paceville: The Heart of Nightlife

Paceville, located in the heart of St. Julian's, is Malta's premier nightlife destination, renowned for its vibrant energy and diverse entertainment options. This bustling area serves as the focal point for locals and tourists alike who are looking to experience the dynamic Maltese nightlife.

Location and Access

Paceville is situated in the northeastern part of Malta, adjacent to St. George's Bay. It's easily accessible from various parts of the island via public transportation—buses frequently run to and from major locations including Valletta, Sliema, and the Malta International Airport. For those driving, there are several public parking areas and private parking garages in and around Paceville. Taxis and rideshare services are readily available, offering a convenient option for late-night travel.

Things to Do in Paceville

Paceville offers an array of activities that cater to all tastes:

1. **Nightclubs and Bars:** The area boasts a wide range of clubs and bars, each offering unique themes, music genres, and atmospheres. From dance clubs with DJ sets playing the latest hits to quieter lounges where you can enjoy a cocktail, there's something for everyone.

2. **Live Music Venues:** Several venues offer live music, featuring both local and international bands. These spots are perfect for those who prefer live performances over recorded music.

3. **Casinos:** For those feeling lucky, Paceville is home to some of Malta's most popular casinos. These spots not only offer a variety of games but also serve as entertainment hubs with bars and occasional live shows.

4. Cinemas and Bowling Alleys: For a more relaxed evening, you can visit the cinemas or go bowling. These facilities are modern and well-maintained, providing a fun and leisurely experience.

5. Dining Options: Paceville is also known for its culinary variety, with restaurants and eateries serving everything from quick bites to gourmet meals. The area's food scene includes local Maltese cuisine, as well as international dishes.

Making the Experience Memorable

To truly enjoy Paceville, consider starting your evening with a sunset walk along St. George's Bay before diving into the nightlife. Dress codes vary by venue, so it's wise to check in advance if you're planning a night out at a more upscale club or casino. Additionally, while Paceville is generally safe, as with any busy nightlife area, it's recommended to stay aware of your surroundings and keep personal belongings secure.

Visiting Paceville offers more than just a night out; it's an opportunity to immerse yourself in the lively pulse of Malta's nocturnal offerings. Whether you're dancing the night away, trying your luck at the roulette table, or enjoying a live band, Paceville promises an unforgettable night out filled with excitement and entertainment.

Nightlife and Entertainment: Bars, Clubs, and Live Music

Malta's nightlife scene is as diverse and vibrant as its history and culture, offering a plethora of options for every taste and style. From lively bars and clubs to intimate live music venues, the islands provide a rich tapestry of nighttime entertainment that caters to both locals and tourists.

Geographic and Access Information
The hub of Malta's nightlife is undoubtedly the Paceville district in St. Julian's, known for its dense concentration of nightclubs, bars, and pubs. However, other areas such as Valletta, Sliema, and Buġibba also offer significant nightlife options with their own unique flavors. These areas are well-connected by Malta's public transport system, which includes night buses on key routes. Taxis and rideshare options are plentiful, making it easy to move between different nightlife spots safely and efficiently.

Nightlife and Entertainment Venues

1. **Bars and Pubs:** Malta boasts an array of bars and pubs, ranging from beach bars with a relaxed, laid-back atmosphere to sophisticated wine bars in Valletta's historic buildings. Many bars offer themed nights, happy hours, and live DJ sets, ensuring a lively atmosphere that goes on till the early hours.

2. **Clubs:** For those seeking a high-energy night out, Paceville's clubs are the go-to spots. These clubs frequently host international DJs and themed party nights, attracting a young and energetic crowd. Clubs in Malta typically feature various music genres, including house, techno, hip-hop, and mainstream pop hits.

3. **Live Music:** Live music is an integral part of Malta's entertainment scene. Venues across the islands host performances ranging from jazz and blues to rock and classical. These concerts often

take place in unique settings such as ancient vaults or outdoor public squares, adding to the overall experience.

Activities and Tips for a Memorable Night Out
- **Start with Sunset:** Many bars, especially those along the coast, offer stunning views of the Mediterranean sunset. Starting your evening with a sunset drink can set the tone for a relaxed and enjoyable night out.
- **Explore Different Genres:** Take the opportunity to explore different music scenes within Malta. From live rock bands in gritty bars to elegant classical music concerts in Valletta, there's something to match every musical taste.
- **Safety First:** While Malta is generally safe, it's important to be mindful of your surroundings, especially late at night. Stick to well-lit areas and travel in groups when possible.

- **Respect Local Customs:** While Maltese nightlife is quite liberal, it's good practice to respect local customs and dress codes, particularly when visiting more upscale or traditional venues.

In addition exploring Malta's nightlife offers an array of choices for every preference. Below are some recommended bars and clubs across the island, each offering unique experiences from lively dance floors to cozy, atmospheric settings.

1. Hugo's Terrace
- **Location:** St. George's Road, St. Julian's, Malta
- **Phone:** +356 2137 6767
- **Price Range:** $15-$30 per person

Hugo's Terrace is well-known for its vibrant atmosphere and stunning views of St. George's Bay. It's a great spot for cocktails and has a lively dance floor with frequent DJ performances.

2. The Thirsty Barber

- **Location:** Ball Street, Paceville, St. Julian's, Malta
- **Phone:** +356 2738 2326
- **Price Range:** $10-$25 per person

Known as Malta's first prohibition-style bar, The Thirsty Barber offers a unique twist with its hidden entrance and 1920s-inspired cocktails. The ambiance is perfect for those looking for a night of fun with a historical twist.

3. Bridge Bar

- **Location:** St. Ursula Street, Valletta, Malta
- **Phone:** +356 9963 3716
- **Price Range:** $10-$20 per person

Bridge Bar offers a more laid-back vibe with jazz nights and a picturesque setting in the heart of Valletta. It's ideal for a relaxed evening enjoying live music under the stars.

4. Club Phoenix

- **Location:** Gianpula Village, Limits of Rabat, Malta
- **Phone:** +356 9949 4881
- **Price Range:** $20-$40 per person

Set in the countryside away from the typical tourist spots, Club Phoenix is part of the larger Gianpula Village, which hosts several clubs and bars. It features a large outdoor area with regular live DJ sets and themed party nights.

5. Sky Club

- **Location:** Dragonara Road, St. Julian's, Malta
- **Phone:** +356 2138 1000
- **Price Range:** $15-$35 per person

One of the largest indoor clubs in Malta, Sky Club is perfect for electronic music enthusiasts. The club boasts state-of-the-art sound systems and lighting, hosting renowned international DJs.

These venues provide just a glimpse into the diverse nightlife of Malta. Whether you're looking for a high-energy club to dance the night away or a more subdued bar for a relaxed evening, Malta offers a range of options to suit any night owl's preferences. Remember to check each venue's calendar for special events and dress codes to make the most of your nightlife experience in Malta.

Casino and Entertainment Options

Malta is not only known for its rich history and beautiful landscapes but also for its vibrant casino and entertainment scene. Offering a variety of gaming and entertainment options, the island's casinos are prime destinations for those seeking excitement and a touch of glamour during their stay.

Location and Access

Most of Malta's main casinos are strategically located in tourist-frequented areas, making them easily accessible:

1. Dragonara Casino is situated at Dragonara Road, St. Julian's, within the premises of the historic Dragonara Palace. Easily accessible by bus or taxi, it's a focal point in Malta's nightlife hub.

2. Casino Malta is located in St. George's Bay, St. Julian's. It is part of the InterContinental Hotel complex, which is well-served by public transport and offers ample parking.

3. Portomaso Casino resides within the luxurious Portomaso Marina, offering not just gaming but also a taste of the high life with yachts docked just steps away.

Gaming and Entertainment

Each casino in Malta offers a wide range of gaming options including slots, poker, blackjack, roulette, and many other table games. Here's what you can expect:

- Dragonara Casino combines elegance with a comprehensive gaming experience, offering over 300 slot machines and a variety of table games. It's also known for hosting major poker tournaments.
- Casino Malta is the largest on the island and provides a vibrant gaming floor with state-of-the-art slot machines and a

dynamic array of table games. They also offer an immersive sports betting area.
- Portomaso Casino is smaller but offers a more intimate setting with a focus on luxury. Its gaming floors are equipped with a selection of table games and slots, and it is renowned for its high-stake poker games.

Beyond Gaming

Casinos in Malta are not just about gambling; they provide a full entertainment experience:

- **Live Entertainment:** Enjoy live music, performances, and international DJ sets that transform these venues into lively entertainment complexes during the evenings.
- **Dining Options:** Each casino features a range of dining facilities, from upscale restaurants to casual eateries, catering to all tastes and occasions.

- **Special Events:** Casinos often host special events, themed nights, and more, providing a diverse entertainment calendar that caters to both locals and tourists.

Tips for Visiting

To make the most of your visit:

- **Check Age Restrictions:** Ensure you meet the age requirement of 18 years or older, with a valid ID to enter.
- **Dress Code:** Most casinos have a smart-casual dress code, especially during the evening.
- **Set a Budget:** Decide on a spending limit beforehand to enjoy responsibly.

Visiting a casino in Malta offers more than just the thrill of gambling; it's a comprehensive entertainment experience that combines luxury, excitement, and top-notch hospitality services.

Mediterraneo Marine Park and Splash & Fun Water Park

Malta offers a delightful range of family-friendly activities, and among these, the Mediterraneo Marine Park and Splash & Fun Water Park stand out as premier destinations for both educational and splash-filled fun.

Mediterraneo Marine Park

Location and Access: Situated in Baħar iċ-Ċagħaq on the northeastern coast of Malta, the Marine Park is easily accessible via public transport with several bus routes serving the area directly from major locations such as Valletta and Sliema. For those driving, there is ample parking available onsite.

Activities and Educational Experiences: The Mediterraneo Marine Park is a phenomenal place where visitors can interact with various marine animals and learn about marine conservation. The park offers:

- **Dolphin and Sea Lion Shows:** These shows not only entertain but also educate audiences about the behaviors and needs of these intelligent creatures.
- **Parrot Shows:** Adding a splash of color and fun, these shows highlight the intelligence of parrots, engaging visitors with tricks and talking performances.
- **Swim with Dolphins:** For a truly unforgettable experience, visitors can swim with dolphins under the guidance of professional trainers, learning about dolphin behavior and conservation efforts.
- **Educational Tours:** The park conducts guided tours that educate visitors on the care, diet, and conservation of the marine animals housed there.

Splash & Fun Water Park

Location and Access: Adjacent to the Marine Park, this water park is located on the coast road in Baħar iċ-Ċagħaq. It shares the same accessibility features as the Marine Park, making it convenient for visitors to enjoy both attractions in a single trip.

Activities and Attractions: Designed to provide a thrilling day out for families and thrill-seekers, the water park features:

- **Various Slides:** From high-speed slides to more gentle options for younger children, there's something to suit every thrill level.
- **Wave Pool:** Simulating a beach experience, the wave pool is a favorite for all ages, perfect for bobbing along on the waves.
- **Lazy River:** For a more relaxing experience, the lazy river offers a slow and enjoyable ride around the park with views of all the attractions.
- **Children's Play Area:** Specifically designed for younger visitors, this area is safer and offers water fun at a more suitable pace.

Making the Experience Memorable
- **Picnic Areas and Restaurants:** Both parks have several food outlets and picnic areas where families can enjoy a meal or a snack between activities.
- **Season Passes and Group Discounts:** For regular visitors, season passes offer great value, while group discounts make it more accessible for larger parties.
- **Safety First:** Both parks prioritize safety with lifeguards on duty and all necessary safety equipment and procedures in place.

A visit to the Mediterraneo Marine Park and Splash & Fun Water Park in Malta provides not just entertainment but also educational opportunities that raise awareness about marine life and environmental conservation. These parks offer a blend of learning and leisure, making them perfect destinations for families looking to make the most of Malta's sunny days.

Festivals and Events: A Year-Round Guide

Malta, a vibrant archipelago in the Mediterranean, offers a rich tapestry of festivals and events throughout the year that reflect its diverse culture and history. These events range from religious festivities and seasonal feasts to music, arts, and food festivals, providing endless entertainment and learning opportunities for visitors.

Carnival (February/March): Held annually in Valletta and various towns across Malta and Gozo, the Maltese Carnival is known for its colorful parades, elaborate floats, and masquerades.

- **Location and Access:** The main activities are in Valletta, easily accessible by public transportation from any part of the island.
- **Activities:** Attendees can watch stunning float parades, participate in costume balls, and enjoy traditional Maltese music and dance.

Malta International Fireworks Festival (April): This spectacular event is held in Valletta's Grand Harbour but includes multiple locations across the islands.

- **Location and Access:** Best viewed from the Valletta waterfront, accessible via bus or ferry services.
- **Activities:** The festival features local and international fireworks companies competing to put on the most impressive pyrotechnic displays, accompanied by live music and celebrations.

Isle of MTV (June): This free annual music festival, held in Floriana, has become one of Europe's largest.

- **Location and Access:** The Granaries in Floriana, just outside the capital city of Valletta, are easily reachable by bus.
- **Activities:** Featuring performances by top international artists, the event draws large

crowds for a night of energetic music and dance.

Malta Jazz Festival (July): Taking place in Valletta, this festival attracts jazz enthusiasts from around the globe.
- **Location and Access:** Events are primarily held at Ta' Liesse, lower Valletta, which is accessible on foot or by public transit from many parts of Malta.
- **Activities:** Enjoy performances by world-renowned jazz musicians in a scenic harbor setting.

The Feast of Santa Marija (August): One of Malta's most important religious holidays, celebrated with much fervor across the islands, especially in Gozo.
- **Location and Access:** Particularly prominent in the town of Victoria in Gozo, reachable by ferry and then public transport or car.

- **Activities:** Visitors can witness traditional processions, band marches, and the spectacular fireworks that light up the night sky.

Notte Bianca (October): Valletta opens its palaces, museums, and galleries for one night of art, culture, and entertainment.
- **Location and Access:** Throughout Valletta, easily accessible by public transport.
- **Activities:** Explore open museums and galleries, street performances, and concerts, all available till late at night.

Malta International Christmas Choir Festival (December): Choirs from Malta and overseas come together to perform in various venues across the islands.
- **Location and Access:** Performances take place in churches and theatres across

Malta and Gozo, with primary venues often in Valletta.
- **Activities:** Attend beautiful choir performances that range from classical to modern interpretations of Christmas carols.

Attending these festivals offers more than just entertainment; it is an opportunity to immerse yourself in the Maltese culture, meet locals, and participate in traditions that have been celebrated for generations. Each event is set in accessible locations, ensuring that visitors can easily join in the festivities. Whether it's through music, art, or religious observances, Malta's year-round festivals provide unforgettable experiences for all who partake.

CHAPTER 13

Exploring Malta by Traveler Type

Malta, a gem in the heart of the Mediterranean, offers a treasure trove of experiences tailored to different types of travelers. This chapter is dedicated to exploring the distinct ways solo travelers, couples, families, and senior travelers can immerse themselves in Malta's rich tapestry. Each section provides specific insights and recommendations to ensure every traveler feels welcomed and well catered to, regardless of their travel style or needs.

For solo adventurers, we delve into essential tips and safe practices to help you navigate Malta confidently and securely. From finding cozy cafes and joining group tours to exploring the nightlife safely, this guide aims to empower solo explorers with all the necessary tools for a fulfilling journey.

Couples looking for a romantic getaway will discover Malta's most enchanting spots. Whether it's sunset views from the Dingli Cliffs or a candlelit dinner in Mdina, this section highlights activities and locations that spark romance and create lasting memories.

Families visiting Malta will find a wealth of attractions suitable for all ages. This part of the chapter outlines the best kid-friendly activities, from interactive museums to public parks and family-oriented dining options, ensuring that every family member enjoys their time to the fullest.

Lastly, for senior travelers, the focus is on accessibility and leisure options that cater to comfort and ease of travel. From leisurely walks in the San Anton Gardens to accessible tours of historical sites, this section ensures that more seasoned visitors can enjoy Malta's beauty without inconvenience.

Embark on this chapter to uncover Malta's diverse appeal, ensuring that no matter your age or travel style, you'll find something that resonates deeply, making your visit truly unforgettable.

Solo Travelers: Tips and Safe Practices

Malta, with its rich historical backdrop and vibrant culture, presents a fantastic destination for solo travelers looking to explore and immerse themselves in new experiences. This section provides essential tips and safe practices to help you navigate the island independently, ensuring a secure and enjoyable visit.

Getting to and Around Malta

Malta International Airport is the gateway to the island, located in Luqa. From here, solo travelers can easily access various parts of the island via public transport, rental cars, or taxis. The compact size of Malta makes it easy to explore. Buses are reliable and cover extensive routes, while renting a scooter can offer more flexibility and a scenic way to see the countryside.

Accommodations

For solo travelers, staying in hostels or guesthouses in Valletta or Sliema offers not only budget-friendly options but also opportunities to meet fellow travelers. These areas are well-policed and centrally located, providing safe environments and easy access to main attractions.

Safety Tips

1. **Stay Connected:** Always keep your phone charged and data-enabled to access maps and communicate in case of emergencies.

2. **Be Aware of Your Surroundings:** Especially at night, stick to well-lit and populated areas.

3. **Keep Essentials Secure:** Use a money belt or a secure cross-body bag to keep your valuables safe from pickpockets, particularly in busy tourist spots.

Things to Do

- **Historical Tours:** Join guided tours to explore Malta's rich history. From the ancient streets of Mdina to the grandeur of Valletta, guided tours are not only informative but also a way to meet people.

- **Outdoor Activities:** Engage in hiking or join group kayaking trips around the stunning Blue Lagoon. These activities offer the dual benefit of adventure and companionship.
- **Cultural Experiences:** Participate in local workshops or cooking classes to learn more about Maltese cuisine and crafts.
- **Nightlife:** Visit the bustling nightlife scene in Paceville safely by sticking to reputable venues and keeping an eye on your drink.

Making the Experience Memorable

- **Photography Walks:** Malta offers picturesque landscapes and urban settings perfect for photography. Joining a photography group or club can enhance your experience and provide safety in numbers.
- **Café Culture:** Spend time in local cafés where you can enjoy Maltese pastizzi while reading or planning your next

activity. It's a relaxing way to enjoy Malta's local flavors and observe daily life.

By following these tips and embracing all that Malta has to offer, solo travelers can safely enjoy a rich and fulfilling experience. Whether exploring ancient architecture, engaging in water sports, or simply enjoying the local cuisine at a seaside café, Malta offers a warm and inviting atmosphere for everyone.

Couples: Romantic Spots and Activities

Malta, with its stunning landscapes and historical richness, provides the perfect backdrop for couples seeking both romance and adventure. This guide explores a variety of romantic spots and activities across the island that are ideal for creating memorable experiences together.

Getting to and Around

Malta is well-connected by its international airport, located near Valletta. For couples, renting a car is perhaps the most convenient way to explore the island at your own pace. Alternatively, the public bus service offers extensive routes that are economical and effective for reaching major attractions.

Romantic Spots

1. **Mdina:** Known as the "Silent City," Mdina offers a magical backdrop with its ancient walls and quiet, narrow streets. A walk through Mdina at sunset, when the golden hues light up the

limestone walls, creates an unforgettable romantic atmosphere. It's easily accessible by bus or car from any part of the island.

2. **Dingli Cliffs:** Offering some of the most spectacular sea views, the Dingli Cliffs are perfect for a scenic walk at sunset. Located on the western coast, these cliffs can be reached by a direct bus from Valletta or by car. The serene surroundings make it a great spot for a quiet picnic or simply to admire the vast views of the Mediterranean.

3. **Comino's Blue Lagoon:** For a day trip, visit the crystal-clear waters of the Blue Lagoon on Comino Island. Boats depart regularly from Malta and Gozo, providing a short and scenic ride to this beautiful spot. Spend a day swimming, snorkeling, and lounging on the boat decks or the small beach.

Activities for Couples

- **Boat Trips:** Private charters or group boat tours can be arranged from Sliema, St. Julian's, or Valletta. Explore the coastlines, discover secluded bays, and enjoy the intimate setting of a boat ride at sunset.

- **Wine Tasting:** Visit one of Malta's wineries, such as Meridiana or Marsovin, which offer tours and tastings. Located in central Malta, these wineries are accessible by car and provide a delightful outing where you can learn about local viticulture and enjoy the flavors of Maltese wines.

- **Spa Days:** Several luxury hotels and resorts offer spa services where couples can indulge in massages and treatments for a day of relaxation. The Corinthia Hotel in St. George's Bay is renowned for its spa facilities and offers packages for couples.

Making the Experience Memorable

- **Dinner with a View:** Malta is filled with restaurants that offer dining with scenic views. Consider a waterfront dinner in Valletta or a cliff-top restaurant in Mellieha. These locations not only provide exquisite meals but also enchanting atmospheres for a romantic evening.
- **Photography Sessions:** Book a professional photography session to capture your moments in Malta. Whether it's in the baroque settings of Valletta or the rugged landscapes of Gozo, these photos will be cherished reminders of your journey together.

Each of these destinations and activities has been chosen to enhance the romantic experience in Malta, offering couples not just places to see, but memories to build. Enjoy the blend of adventure, relaxation, and romance as you explore the island's charms together.

Family Adventures: Kid-Friendly Attractions and Dining

Malta offers an abundance of family-friendly activities and dining options that make it an ideal destination for a vacation with children. From interactive museums to expansive parks and specialized children's menus, the island caters to the needs of families looking for a blend of fun, learning, and relaxation.

Locations and Access

- **Malta National Aquarium:** Located in Qawra, within St. Paul's Bay area, this aquarium is accessible by multiple bus routes from various parts of the island. It provides an engaging experience with marine life exhibits and interactive zones perfect for children.
- **Playmobil FunPark:** Situated in Hal Far, this park is best reached by car or taxi as public transport options are limited. It offers a playful environment where

children can interact with Playmobil setups and enjoy outdoor play areas.

Things to Do

- **Visit Popeye Village:** Originally built as a movie set for the film 'Popeye', this fun park is now one of the most beloved attractions for families. Located in Mellieha, it's easily reachable by bus or car. Children can enjoy boat rides, puppet shows, and playhouses, all set in the colorful and whimsical village.

- **Exploration at Esplora Interactive Science Centre:** Located in Kalkara, Esplora offers a hands-on science experience with numerous exhibits, workshops, and a planetarium. It's a short drive from Valletta and accessible by bus. The center makes learning fun and engaging for kids of all ages.

Dining Options

Many restaurants in Malta are family-friendly, offering special menus for children and facilities such as high chairs and play areas. Here are a few recommendations:

- **Sharma Ethnic Cuisines:** Located in Mdina, this restaurant offers a diverse menu that caters to various dietary needs, including options for children. The setting is comfortable, with spacious seating ideal for families.
- **The Boat House Restaurant:** Situated in Xlendi, Gozo, this restaurant provides high-quality seafood and a kid-friendly menu right by the sea. It's an excellent spot for families to enjoy a meal after exploring Gozo's charming coastal areas.

Making the Experience Memorable

- **Interactive Tours:** Engage in family-oriented tours that often include scavenger hunts, historical storytelling, and hands-on activities that keep children entertained and educated throughout.

- **Outdoor Adventures:** Take advantage of Malta's beautiful landscapes by planning a day of hiking or birdwatching at places like Ghadira Nature Reserve. Such activities offer children a chance to learn about nature and wildlife in a direct and engaging manner.

- **Beach Time:** Visit Malta's sandy beaches, such as Golden Bay and Mellieha Bay, which are perfect for families. These beaches offer clean, shallow waters and plenty of amenities, including lifeguards during the peak season, making them safe and enjoyable for young children.

These locations and activities highlight Malta's commitment to providing a family-friendly environment that enriches the vacation experience for both children and adults.

Senior Travelers: Accessibility and Leisure Options

Malta, with its rich history and serene landscapes, offers a welcoming environment for senior travelers seeking both relaxation and accessible adventures. The island's commitment to accessibility ensures that older visitors can enjoy a full range of activities, from exploring ancient cities to relaxing by the Mediterranean Sea.

Transportation
- **Public Transport:** Malta's public buses are equipped with low-entry steps and dedicated spaces for wheelchair users, making them accessible for seniors with mobility concerns. Key bus routes connect major towns and attractions across the island.
- **Taxis and Car Rentals:** For more personalized travel, taxis are readily available, and several companies offer vehicles adapted for those with limited

mobility. Car rentals with hand controls are also available for those who prefer to drive themselves.

Accessible Attractions

- **Valletta:** Malta's capital is well-equipped for seniors, with smooth, well-maintained streets and plenty of benches. Key attractions like St. John's Co-Cathedral and the Upper Barrakka Gardens offer wheelchair access. Valletta can be reached via public transport from any part of the island or by taxi.

- **Mdina:** Known as the Silent City, Mdina is another must-visit. While its ancient cobbled streets can be challenging, the main paths are manageable, and the city offers stunning views and quiet, charming cafes. Access is made easier with drop-off points close to the main gate.

Leisure Activities

- **Gardens and Parks:** San Anton Gardens, located in Attard, is a serene spot ideal for leisurely walks amidst lush greenery and shaded paths. The gardens are wheelchair-friendly and provide a peaceful retreat with easy access by public transport or car.

- **Museums:** The National War Museum in Valletta and the Malta Classic Car Museum in Qawra are favorites among senior visitors. Both venues are accessible and provide insights into Malta's rich history and vintage car collections, respectively.

Cultural Experiences

- **Harbour Cruises:** Take a gentle cruise around the Grand Harbour for breathtaking views of Valletta and the Three Cities from the water. These cruises are equipped to assist seniors, with ramps for boarding and comfortable seating.

- **Local Cuisine:** Many Maltese restaurants offer traditional food with the convenience of ground-level entrances and spacious seating. Enjoy a meal of pastizzi (ricotta-filled pastry) or fresh seafood while overlooking the ocean.

Accommodation
- **Senior-Friendly Hotels:** Many hotels in Malta cater to seniors with amenities like ground-floor rooms, lifts, and health facilities. Locations like Sliema and St. Julian's are popular, providing easy access to promenades for morning walks and proximity to cafes and shops.

Making the Experience Memorable
- **Attend Local Festas:** Experience the vibrant local culture by attending a 'festa'

(feast) in one of the towns. These events are full of life with music, fireworks, and processions, and offer a taste of Maltese community spirit.

- **Visit Gozo:** A ferry ride to the quieter island of Gozo offers a change of pace with its quaint villages and stunning natural landscapes. Ferries are equipped to handle mobility aids, making the trip comfortable for seniors.

This guide ensures that senior travelers can enjoy Malta's beauty and charm in comfort and style, making their visit a memorable and hassle-free experience.

CHAPTER 14

Day Trips and Extended Excursions

Exploring Malta offers an array of delightful day trips and extended excursions that reveal the island's rich tapestry of history, culture, and natural beauty. This chapter serves as a guide to effectively plan and enjoy these outings, whether you're venturing out from the bustling streets of Valletta or the tranquil villages of Gozo.

We delve into the essentials of orchestrating day trips from Malta's major cities, ensuring you can seamlessly reach the island's most coveted destinations. Whether you opt for the comfort and knowledge of guided tours or the freedom of self-guided explorations, this section provides practical tips and insightful advice to enhance your journey.

From the ancient city of Mdina to the azure waters of the Blue Lagoon in Comino, Malta offers experiences that cater to every type of traveler. Each excursion is an opportunity to immerse yourself in the local culture, indulge in traditional Maltese cuisine, and create memories that last a lifetime. This chapter will prepare you to choose the right adventures that align with your interests and travel style, making every day in Malta a unique exploration.

Planning Day Trips from Major Cities

Exploring Malta through day trips from its major cities—Valletta, Mdina, and Sliema—provides a splendid opportunity to discover the diverse attractions of the island without the need to relocate constantly. These excursions are designed to maximize your experience, allowing you to immerse deeply in the local culture and history within a manageable timeframe.

Starting from Valletta, the capital city, travelers can embark on journeys to nearby highlights such as the historic Three Cities or the picturesque fishing village of Marsaxlokk. Public buses offer frequent services to these destinations, making them easily accessible and budget-friendly. Alternatively, for those who prefer a more personalized experience, various local tour companies offer guided excursions that include transportation, guided tours, and sometimes even meals.

From Mdina, the old capital, venturing into the northern regions is highly recommended. The scenic routes are perfect for driving, and renting a car for the day could provide the freedom to explore at your own pace. Key stops might include the Crafts Village at Ta' Qali or the sweeping beaches of Mellieha Bay, where activities range from sunbathing and swimming to windsurfing and kitesurfing.

Sliema serves as a fantastic base for those looking to enjoy both the urban aspects of Malta and its natural landscapes. Ferries from Sliema can take you directly to Valletta, and from there, you can join boat trips to the Blue Lagoon on Comino island—famous for its crystal-clear waters and excellent snorkeling opportunities.

Each of these trips can be tailored to fit personal interests, whether you're drawn to Malta's rich history, its vibrant local markets, or its stunning coastal walks. With each journey, ensure to engage with local guides, try traditional Maltese cuisine, and take the time to soak in the serene views, making each day trip a memorable chapter of your Maltese adventure.

Guided Tours vs. Self-Guided Explorations

In Malta, travelers have the enriching option to choose between guided tours and self-guided explorations, each offering distinct experiences tailored to different types of adventurers. This choice significantly affects how one experiences the rich tapestry of history, culture, and natural beauty that Malta presents.

Guided tours in Malta are particularly advantageous for those who prefer a structured approach to travel. These tours are often led by knowledgeable local guides who provide in-depth insights into the historical context and cultural significance of each site. For example, guided tours of Valletta's historic streets or the ancient city of Mdina can enrich your understanding with stories and facts that might elude the casual visitor. These tours can be accessed through numerous local and online agencies, offering everything from walking tours and specialized museum visits to boat tours around the archipelago.

On the other hand, self-guided explorations in Malta appeal to those who seek a more flexible and intimate encounter with their surroundings. This option allows travelers to move at their own pace and according to their personal interests. For instance, one might choose to spend a leisurely day exploring the coastal paths of the Dingli Cliffs or the rural landscapes of Gozo. Getting around for self-guided tours is facilitated by Malta's comprehensive public transport system, which connects major towns and cities to popular tourist spots, or through car rentals that offer the freedom to explore more secluded areas.

Both types of travel experiences offer unique ways to engage with Malta's offerings. Guided tours provide a depth of knowledge and ease of access, especially beneficial for those visiting complex historical sites or participating in activities like scuba diving or rock climbing, where expert guidance enhances safety and enjoyment. Meanwhile, self-guided tours are perfect for those who wish to immerse themselves in local culture at a leisurely pace, perhaps discovering hidden gems along the way that are not typically included in structured tour itineraries.

Ultimately, whether opting for the enriching narrative of a guided tour or the personal discovery of a self-guided adventure, Malta offers a wealth of activities and sites. Each visitor can choose based on their travel style to create memorable experiences in this vibrant Mediterranean landscape.

In addition, for those planning to explore Malta through guided tours, here are some reputable options that cater to various interests, from historical excursions to scenic adventures. Each company provides knowledgeable guides and comprehensive tours that can enhance your experience on the island.

1. **Colours of Malta**
   - **Address:** Triq il-Merghat, Zone 3 Central Business District, Birkirkara, CBD 3110, Malta
   - **Phone:** +356 2145 0707
   - **Email:** info@coloursmalta.com
   - **Website:**(http://www.coloursmalta.com)
   - **Price Range:** $30 - $150 per person

Offers customized tours that include historical sites like Mdina and Valletta, cultural experiences with local crafts, and culinary tours that explore traditional Maltese cuisine.

2. **Malta Tour Guides**
   - **Address:** 71, Old College Street, Sliema SLM 1378, Malta
   - **Phone:** +356 9986 3339
   - **Email:** info@maltatourguides.com

- **Website:** (http://www.maltatourguides.com)
- **Price Range**: $45 - $200 per person

Specializes in comprehensive historical tours, offering insights into Malta's rich history at key archaeological sites and museums. They also provide themed tours such as WWII in Malta, Knights of St. John, and architectural tours of Valletta.

3. **Best of Malta**
   - **Address:** 23, Strait Street, Valletta, VLT 1432, Malta
   - **Phone:** +356 9999 1234
   - **Email:** bookings@bestofmalta.com
   - **Website:** (http://www.bestofmalta.com)
   - **Price Range:** $50 - $250 per person

Offers luxury tours that include private yacht charters around the Maltese archipelago, exclusive visits to private palaces and gardens not normally open to the public, and custom itineraries that can include helicopter tours for unique aerial views of the islands.

4. Heritage Malta Tours
- **Address:** HM07, Valletta, Malta
- **Phone:** +356 2295 4000
- **Email:** info@heritagemalta.org
- **Website:**(http://www.heritagemalta.org)
- **Price Range:** $15 - $100 per person

Operated by the national agency for museums, conservation practices, and cultural heritage. Tours focus on Malta's prehistoric temples, historical fortifications, and the rich collections within national museums. They often include special access to restricted areas and expert commentary from conservation specialists.

These tours cater to a range of interests from deep historical dives to luxurious and unique experiences, ensuring that every visitor finds something that will enrich their visit to Malta.

CHAPTER 15

Itineraries

Navigating through the myriad of attractions in Malta can be as delightful as it is daunting, especially for first-time visitors or those looking to maximize their time. This chapter on itineraries is crafted to guide you through organizing your stay with various well-planned schedules that cater to different travel durations and interests. From quick three-day getaways that cover the highlights of Malta's historical and cultural sites to comprehensive week-long explorations that delve deeper into the archipelago's offerings, these itineraries are designed to enhance your experience.

For those with a specific focus, we also provide specialized itineraries tailored to adventures that get your adrenaline pumping, cultural immersions that explore the depth of Maltese history and art, or relaxation-themed tours that allow for leisurely days spent by the sea or pampered in luxury. Each itinerary suggestion balances popular tourist spots with hidden gems, ensuring a rich and rewarding visit.

The following sections will lay out these varied itineraries with practical advice on how to fit them into your travel plans, whether you are navigating alone, as a couple, or with a family. These guides aim to not only inspire your journey but also streamline your planning process, allowing you to immerse fully in the vibrant life and stunning landscapes of Malta. Each suggested plan is built to be flexible yet comprehensive, ensuring that every traveler can find their perfect pace and preference covered in the pages to come.

Quick Getaways: 3-Day Itineraries

Quick getaways in Malta offer a remarkable opportunity to immerse in the rich tapestry of history, culture, and natural beauty this island nation boasts, all within a compact three-day itinerary. Perfect for those who want to experience the essence of Malta without spending too much time, these itineraries are designed to cover key attractions and provide memorable experiences.

Day one typically starts in the capital city, Valletta. Recognized as a UNESCO World Heritage site, Valletta is accessible via Malta International Airport, with frequent direct bus services and taxis available to take you into the city. Spend your morning wandering the storied streets of Valletta, visiting landmarks like St. John's Co-Cathedral and the Upper Barrakka Gardens, which offers panoramic views of the Grand Harbour.

On the second day, head to the ancient city of Mdina, known as the Silent City. Buses run regularly from Valletta to Mdina, taking about half an hour. Explore the narrow alleys, visit the imposing bastions, and perhaps stop at the Mdina Experience for an audio-visual recount of the city's history. Close your day with a trip to nearby Rabat to explore St. Paul's Catacombs.

The final day can be dedicated to the islands of Gozo and Comino. Ferry services from Cirkewwa on Malta to Gozo take about 25 minutes, and once in Gozo, you can rent a car or use local buses to explore. Highlights include the Ggantija Temples and the stunning Azure Window site, though the original arch collapsed in 2017. Do not miss taking a short boat trip from Gozo to the turquoise waters of the Blue Lagoon on Comino, ideal for a relaxing swim or snorkeling.

Each day packs in diverse activities and sights, from historical tours to leisurely strolls and relaxing by the sea, ensuring that every moment of your stay is captivating. Despite the short stay, these itineraries ensure a comprehensive experience of Malta's unique offerings, making every trip memorable and enriching. This guide aims to provide all the necessary details to make your travel seamless and enjoyable without the need for extensive planning.

Weeklong Explorations: Comprehensive 7-Day Tours

Embarking on a weeklong exploration of Malta allows visitors to delve deep into the island's rich history, stunning landscapes, and vibrant culture. This comprehensive 7-day tour is meticulously crafted to ensure travelers can experience the very best of Malta, from its bustling cities to tranquil coastlines.

The journey begins in Valletta, Malta's capital, where travelers can land at Malta International Airport. Easily accessible from major European airports, the city is a short ride from the airport by bus, taxi, or rental car. Valletta, a UNESCO World Heritage site, offers a dense concentration of historic architecture, including the majestic St. John's Co-Cathedral and the grandiose Grand Master's Palace. Spend the first day and a half exploring the city's museums, gardens, and the bustling Republic Street.

On the third day, venture to the ancient former capital of Mdina, known as the "Silent City," for its quiet and atmospheric streets. Explore medieval architecture, visit the Mdina Dungeon, and enjoy stunning views of the island from the city walls. A short trip to nearby Rabat to see St. Paul's Catacombs is also recommended.

Mid-week, take a ferry from Cirkewwa to the island of Gozo. The ferry ride offers scenic views and takes about 25 minutes. In Gozo, visit the Ġgantija Temples, some of the oldest free-standing structures in the world, and wander through the charming streets of Victoria, the capital. Don't miss the stunning scenery of Dwejra Bay, formerly home to the now-collapsed Azure Window.

Day five calls for a day of leisure in Gozo, with options for scuba diving, hiking, or simply relaxing on one of the island's many beaches. In the evening, enjoy a meal at one of Gozo's excellent seafood restaurants.

Returning to Malta, spend the sixth day at the Blue Grotto on the south coast, accessible by bus from Valletta. Take a boat tour to explore the sea caverns and rock formations, followed by a visit to the nearby fishing village of Marsaxlokk to explore its colorful market and waterfront eateries.

Conclude your week with a visit to the Three Cities across the Grand Harbour from Valletta. Explore the maritime history of Vittoriosa, walk through the quiet streets of Cospicua, and finish in Senglea at the tip of the peninsula for panoramic views of the harbor. This itinerary ensures a full experience of all that Malta has to offer, blending historical exploration with leisure and scenic beauty, making every moment memorable.

Specialized Itineraries: Adventure, Culture, and Relaxation

Malta offers an enriching tapestry of experiences suitable for every type of traveler, with itineraries specially tailored for adventure seekers, culture enthusiasts, and those in search of relaxation. These specialized itineraries are designed to make the most of Malta's diverse attractions, ensuring a memorable journey tailored to personal interests and preferences.

For adventure enthusiasts, Malta's landscape provides a natural playground ripe for exploration. Located in the Mediterranean, Malta is easily accessible from major European cities, typically less than a three-hour flight. Upon arrival at Malta International Airport, adventure seekers can begin their journey in the northwest part of the island, where activities range from rock climbing at the rugged cliffs of Mgarr and the Sannat cliffs in Gozo to scuba diving in the crystal-clear waters surrounding the archipelago. Each location is accessible via a short bus ride or a car rental that allows for flexible travel schedules. Culture seekers will find Malta's rich history captivating, with a plethora of sites that are steeped in history from the Neolithic to the modern era. Starting in the capital city of Valletta, a UNESCO World Heritage Site, travelers can immerse themselves in the city's baroque architecture, visit the opulent St. John's Co-Cathedral, and explore the grand halls of the National Museum of Archaeology. From Valletta, a simple bus ride or a leisurely ferry trip can take visitors to the Three Cities, where the blend of medieval and modern architecture tells the stories of Malta's maritime past.

For those looking to unwind, Malta's specialized itineraries focused on relaxation capitalize on the island's serene beaches and luxurious spa resorts. The northern region of the island, particularly Mellieha Bay, offers expansive sandy beaches that are perfect for sunbathing, gentle swims, or simply enjoying a sunset. The area is a short taxi or bus ride away from the airport, making it easily accessible for travelers. Additionally, the island of Comino's Blue Lagoon is a must-visit for its tranquil waters ideal for snorkeling and relaxation, accessible by a regular ferry service from Malta and Gozo.

Each of these itineraries provides ample opportunities to delve into Malta's offerings deeply, ensuring that whether you're scaling cliffs, wandering through ancient streets, or lounging by the sea, your time in Malta is well-spent. The strategic location of activities along with Malta's compact size allows travelers to maximize their visit without long travel times, making it possible to enjoy a rich mix of experiences tailored to personal tastes and interests. This approach ensures a holistic experience of Malta, tailored to enrich each visitor's travel preferences while offering convenient access and a wealth of options to enhance their stay.

CHAPTER 16

Essential Information and Services

Embarking on a journey to Malta as a tourist presents a vibrant palette of experiences, each demanding a certain level of preparation and knowledge to fully enjoy. This chapter serves as your gateway to crucial insights and information that ensure a smooth and enriching visit to the archipelago. From understanding common travel scams and how to steer clear of them, to familiarizing yourself with emergency contacts that could prove invaluable in urgent situations, this section is designed to prepare you for the unexpected and the anticipated alike.

Moreover, it delves into practical aspects such as navigating the local communication landscape—highlighting the best options for SIM cards and internet access to keep you connected. It also respects the diverse needs of travelers, discussing LGBTQ+ travel considerations that help everyone feel welcome and safe. The chapter goes on to explore the scenic drives and road trip routes that offer breathtaking views and memorable experiences along Malta's picturesque roads.

Additionally, it provides a balanced view of spending your time and money wisely in Malta, contrasting free tourist attractions with paid ones, ensuring that you can make informed choices regardless of your budget. Finally, it rounds out with a guide to the most useful apps and websites that transform your mobile device into a personal tour guide and travel planner, making every moment in Malta as effortless as it is enjoyable.

With these tools and knowledge at your disposal, you are set to navigate Malta's rich landscapes and cultural tapestries with confidence and curiosity. Whether you're mapping out a day filled with free museums and historical sites or planning a luxurious evening at a high-end attraction, this chapter is your starting point for a well-rounded Maltese adventure.

Travel Scams and How to Avoid Them

When visiting Malta, it's essential to be aware of common travel scams to ensure your trip remains memorable for all the right reasons. Unfortunately, like many popular tourist destinations, Malta is not immune to schemes that target unsuspecting visitors. The good news is, with the right information, you can easily spot and avoid these pitfalls.

Most travel scams in Malta revolve around overcharging, especially in taxis and at informal vendor stalls. Taxi drivers might not always use the meter and can charge inflated prices, particularly from the airport to major tourist spots. To counter this, always ensure the meter is running or negotiate a price before starting your journey. It's also wise to use reputable taxi companies or ride-sharing apps where prices are standard and transparent.

Another common tactic involves street vendors or unofficial tour guides offering seemingly exclusive deals that turn out to be overpriced or bogus. They might approach you at busy landmarks offering guided tours or 'skip-the-line' access. While many of these offers are legitimate, always check for official identification and compare prices before committing your money.

Additionally, be cautious with your possessions, especially in crowded areas like festivals or public transport, where pickpocketing can occur. It's advisable to use money belts or anti-theft bags and keep a close watch on your belongings.

For the best experiences in Malta, planning is key:
- Use official websites and verified platforms to book tours and activities.
- Check online reviews and forums to hear other travelers' experiences and tips.

- Familiarize yourself with the local area and typical costs for services like dining and transportation to avoid being overcharged.

By staying informed and vigilant, you can avoid common travel scams and enjoy the rich culture, stunning architecture, and warm hospitality Malta has to offer. Whether exploring the ancient streets of Valletta, relaxing by the blue lagoon, or tasting local Maltese cuisine, knowing these tips will help make your trip safe and enjoyable.

Emergency Services and Contacts

When traveling to Malta, it's crucial to be aware of the emergency services available to ensure a safe and secure visit. Malta, like many European countries, has a well-established system for handling emergencies, offering tourists and residents alike peace of mind during their stay.

In Malta, the central emergency phone number is 112. This number can be dialed free of charge from any phone, including mobile phones, even without a SIM card. The 112 service is equipped to handle police, medical, and fire emergencies and can direct callers to the appropriate services based on their needs. English is widely spoken in Malta, so communication during an emergency should not be a concern.

For non-emergency medical needs, Malta has several health centers spread throughout the island. These are typically located in major towns and cities, providing access to medical care for less urgent health issues. Each locality in Malta typically has a health center or a clinic where basic medical services are available. The Mater Dei Hospital, located in Msida, is the main hospital and offers comprehensive medical services, including emergency and specialized care.

In terms of police services, Malta has police stations located in various towns and districts. Tourists can approach these stations for any legal issues, reporting crimes, or even seeking general assistance related to safety. The Maltese police are known for being approachable and helpful, reflecting the island's generally low crime rate and high safety standards.

For tourists driving in Malta, it's important to know that in the event of a road accident, the European emergency number 112 should also be contacted. Additionally, it's advisable to have contact information for roadside assistance if renting a car, as this information is usually provided by rental agencies.

Understanding local emergency protocols is also part of a safe trip. In hotels, information about emergency exits and procedures is typically available in the rooms or provided at check-in. It's a good idea to familiarize yourself with this information, especially if staying in older buildings or in rural areas.

For those venturing into natural areas, like hiking in Malta's scenic landscapes, it's wise to inform someone about your plans and expected return time. While Malta is generally safe for outdoor activities, having a mobile phone charged and with you at all times is a precaution that can make a significant difference in emergencies.

Visitors should also be aware of seasonal weather changes that might necessitate special emergency services, especially when participating in water sports and activities during the windy season or visiting remote areas like the cliffs of Dingli and Gozo.

Being aware of and prepared for contacting emergency services in Malta enhances the safety and enjoyment of your visit. Familiarizing yourself with the basic layout of the places you are visiting, knowing how to get help if needed, and understanding the local protocols for handling potential emergencies can all contribute to a memorable and positive experience in Malta.

Communication: SIM Cards and Internet Access

In Malta, staying connected is easy and convenient for travelers thanks to a robust network of cellular services and widespread Internet access. Understanding how to navigate communication options in Malta will enhance your travel experience, allowing you to share memories, navigate routes, and stay informed.

Upon arrival in Malta, travelers can easily purchase a local SIM card from one of the main telecom providers: GO, Melita, or Vodafone. These providers offer competitive rates for calls, SMS, and data packages. SIM cards can be acquired at outlets located in major tourist areas, including the Malta International Airport, Sliema, Valletta, and St. Julian's. Many shops display recognizable signs of these telecom providers, making them easy to locate.

Purchasing a SIM card typically requires a valid passport, and you can choose from various tariffs that suit your length of stay and data needs. The process is straightforward, with staff usually fluent in English to assist you in setting up your new SIM card immediately.

Internet access in Malta is reliable, with numerous WiFi hotspots available throughout the island. Most hotels, cafes, restaurants, and public spaces like libraries and museums offer free WiFi to customers and visitors. For those needing more consistent access to the Internet, portable WiFi routers can be rented from the airport or telecom shops, providing a continuous mobile data connection without the need to rely on public networks.

For travelers exploring Malta, staying connected can enhance your visit significantly. With your own Internet access, navigating the historic streets of Valletta, finding hidden gems in Mdina, or exploring the coastal landscapes becomes easier with access to online maps and local information. Additionally, instant communication capabilities allow for easy bookings and confirmations of tours and tickets to attractions, enhancing your travel efficiency.

Moreover, being able to share your experiences in real-time through social media or communicate with locals and fellow travelers digitally can enrich your interaction with the Maltese culture and its people. Whether it's uploading photos of the stunning Blue Lagoon or sharing your culinary adventures in local Maltese cuisine, enhanced connectivity ensures that you can share and save your travel highlights effortlessly.

Understanding and utilizing the available communication options in Malta can significantly streamline your travel experience. From the moment you land, acquiring a local SIM card or securing Internet access will provide you with the tools needed to explore confidently, stay safe, and make the most of your visit to the enchanting Maltese Islands.

LGBTQ+ Travel Considerations

Malta stands out in the Mediterranean for its progressive stance on LGBTQ+ rights, making it a welcoming destination for travelers seeking both a vibrant cultural experience and a respectful environment. Understanding the local landscape and knowing what Malta offers can help ensure a fulfilling and respectful visit.

Located in the central Mediterranean between Sicily and the North African coast, Malta is accessible by air from major European cities and by ferry from Sicily. Once in Malta, the transportation system comprising buses and taxis facilitates easy travel across the main islands of Malta, Gozo, and Comino.

For LGBTQ+ travelers, Malta offers a variety of activities and spaces that cater to diverse interests. The capital city, Valletta, is a UNESCO World Heritage site with a rich history visible in its ancient fortifications and lively streets. Valletta hosts various cultural events throughout the year, including LGBTQ+ inclusive festivals like Malta Pride, which features a parade, concerts, and parties that showcase the island's inclusive spirit.

Beyond the festivities, LGBTQ+ visitors can explore dedicated bars and clubs primarily located in areas like Paceville and St. Julian's. These venues often host themed nights, drag shows, and other community events that attract a diverse and international crowd.

Culturally, Malta is also home to museums and galleries that offer insights into the island's colorful past and contemporary art scenes. The National Museum of Archaeology in Valletta and the Contemporary Art Spaces in various towns are worth visiting for those interested in the arts.

For those seeking relaxation, Malta's numerous beaches offer a serene escape. Places like Ghajn Tuffieha and Golden Bay are popular for their beautiful views and welcoming atmosphere. For a quieter experience, the smaller island of Gozo provides rustic charm with less commercial development, offering peaceful hiking trails and secluded beaches.

Safety and acceptance are key considerations for any traveler. Malta has enacted pro-LGBTQ+ legislation, including anti-discrimination laws, making it one of the most progressive countries in Europe regarding LGBTQ+ rights. However, as with any destination, it's wise to be aware of your surroundings and adopt a respectful approach towards local customs and interactions.

Travelers are encouraged to connect with local LGBTQ+ organizations for updated information on events and safe spaces. These organizations can provide valuable resources and a connection to the local community, enhancing the travel experience.

Malta presents a unique blend of historical richness, scenic beauty, and a forward-thinking approach to LGBTQ+ inclusion, making it a compelling destination for travelers looking to explore the Mediterranean. From historical tours in Valletta to beach outings and vibrant nightlife, Malta offers an enriching and welcoming atmosphere for all visitors, ensuring a memorable and safe journey.

Road Trip Routes and Scenic Drives

Exploring Malta through its road trip routes and scenic drives presents an exceptional way to appreciate the island's unique landscapes and rich history. With its compact size, Malta offers a variety of routes that are accessible and filled with memorable activities and sights.

Malta's main island, together with its sister islands Gozo and Comino, is situated in the central Mediterranean, south of Sicily and north of Africa. The Malta International Airport serves as the primary gateway for visitors, with regular flights from major European cities. Once on the island, travelers can rent cars directly at the airport or in major cities, allowing for immediate exploration of the scenic routes.

One of the most popular drives is the coastal road from Valletta to the Blue Grotto. This route offers stunning Mediterranean views, passing through picturesque villages like Marsaxlokk, known for its colorful fishing boats and seafood restaurants. The Blue Grotto itself, with its dazzling blue waters, is accessible by a short boat ride, providing an up-close experience of Malta's natural beauty.

Another must-drive route is the road to Dingli Cliffs, the highest point in Malta. The drive along these cliffs affords panoramic views of the open sea and the tiny, uninhabited islet of Filfla. Near Dingli Cliffs, travelers can visit the ancient, megalithic temples of Hagar Qim and Mnajdra, set against the backdrop of the sea.

For those venturing to Gozo, a scenic drive around the island includes stops at the Azure Window ruins, the Inland Sea, and Ramla Bay, famous for its red sand. Gozo's roadways wind through rural landscapes, offering a slower-paced experience compared to the main island. The ferry from Ċirkewwa on Malta to Mġarr on Gozo makes this island easily accessible for those looking to extend their road trip.

In addition to natural and historical sites, Malta's road trips can include culinary stops at local pastizzerias to sample traditional Maltese pastizzi, a flaky pastry filled with ricotta or peas. Each region has its own variations of this beloved snack, making culinary exploration an integral part of the travel experience.

Safety on Malta's roads is enhanced by well-maintained routes and clear signage, catering to drivers who are accustomed to left-hand traffic. Renting a GPS or using a smartphone with local data packages helps in navigating the sometimes narrow and winding roads with confidence.

This journey through Malta's roadways not only reveals the island's spectacular scenery but also intertwines the deep historical roots and vibrant local culture, ensuring a road trip that is both captivating and enlightening. Each drive promises new discoveries, from secluded coves and ancient ruins to lively local festivals, making every journey a unique exploration of this Mediterranean gem.

Free Tourist Attractions

Malta, a small island nation in the heart of the Mediterranean, is abundant with free tourist attractions that offer visitors a deep dive into its rich history, stunning landscapes, and vibrant culture without the need for admission fees. These sites provide a wallet-friendly way to explore the depth and diversity of Maltese heritage and natural beauty.

One of the prime locations for free attractions is the capital city of Valletta, a UNESCO World Heritage site. Here, visitors can stroll through the Upper Barrakka Gardens, which offer a panoramic view of the Grand Harbour, one of the most beautiful harbors in Europe. The gardens are a short walk from the city's main entrance, accessible by public buses that run frequently from various parts of the island. Nearby, the changing of the guards at the Presidential Palace is a ceremonial spectacle that happens once a month and is open to the public at no charge.

Moving north from Valletta, another notable free site is the Mdina Dungeons, located in the ancient capital of Mdina. This old city is a labyrinth of narrow streets that lead to the central cathedral. Although there is a fee to enter the Mdina Cathedral, wandering through the silent city's alleys and viewing its architecture costs nothing. Mdina is easily reached by multiple bus lines from major cities across Malta.

For nature lovers, the Dingli Cliffs offer a breathtaking natural retreat. These cliffs provide not only scenic views of the open sea but also a peaceful hiking trail along the coast. To reach Dingli Cliffs, visitors can take a bus from Valletta to Dingli village and enjoy a short walk to the cliffs. This spot is perfect for sunset views, photography, and picnics, making it a memorable part of any visit to Malta.

On the northeastern coast, Mellieha Bay offers one of Malta's longest sandy beaches. This beach is freely accessible and provides a perfect spot for swimming, sunbathing, and relaxing with a view of the picturesque Mellieha Church set atop the village hill. Public buses serve this route regularly, making it an easy and affordable destination for a day trip.

In addition to these locations, several historical sites across Malta do not charge entrance fees. The Għar Dalam Cave and Museum in Birżebbuġa, where prehistoric animal bones and human artifacts have been found, is free to enter. Similarly, the St. Paul's Catacombs in Rabat offer a glimpse into early Christian burial practices at no cost.

Exploring Malta doesn't require a hefty budget when it comes to attractions. Each of these free sites provides a window into the past and present of the Maltese islands, offering activities and sights that enrich the travel experience. Walking tours, self-guided exploration, and simply enjoying the scenic vistas provide ample opportunity to create lasting memories without the need for expensive tickets or tours.

Paid Tourist Attractions

Malta offers a rich tapestry of paid tourist attractions that cater to diverse interests, from history enthusiasts and art lovers to families and adventure seekers. These attractions are well-maintained and provide structured experiences that delve deep into the cultural, historical, and natural heritage of the islands.

One of the premier paid attractions is the Hal Saflieni Hypogeum, located in Paola. This underground prehistoric burial site, dating back to 4000 B.C., is a UNESCO World Heritage site and offers a fascinating insight into Malta's ancient history. Due to its delicate environment, entry is limited to a small number of visitors per day, making advanced booking essential. Visitors can reach the Hypogeum by bus from Valletta or other major towns. The tour, which lasts about an hour, provides an in-depth look at the architectural skills and artistic achievements of Malta's ancient inhabitants.

Another significant paid attraction is the Fort St. Elmo and the National War Museum in Valletta. The fort offers panoramic views of both Marsamxett and the Grand Harbour. Inside, the museum displays artifacts from Malta's military history, including the famous George Cross awarded to Malta by King George VI for bravery in the Second World War. The fort is easily accessible by public transportation from any part of Malta. Guided tours are available, enhancing the experience with detailed historical narratives and anecdotes.

For those interested in art and architecture, St. John's Co-Cathedral in Valletta is a must-visit. This baroque cathedral, with its opulent interior, features intricate floor tombstones, beautifully detailed frescoes, and Caravaggio's famous painting "The Beheading of Saint John the Baptist." Audio guides are available in multiple languages, providing visitors with a comprehensive understanding of the art, architecture, and religious significance of this majestic site.

Families and marine life enthusiasts might prefer the Malta National Aquarium in Qawra. This modern facility houses Mediterranean, tropical, and freshwater species in well-designed habitats that mimic natural environments. The aquarium is accessible by bus routes connecting to major cities. It offers educational talks and feeding demonstrations, making it a great destination for both adults and children looking to learn more about marine conservation.

Adventure seekers can head to the Malta Falconry Centre, the only one of its kind on the island, where they can observe and interact with various birds of prey. Located in Siggiewi, the center is reachable by a short bus ride from Valletta. It offers flying displays and hands-on experiences, providing insights into the ancient art of falconry set against the backdrop of Malta's rural landscape.

Each of these paid attractions in Malta not only enriches visitors' understanding of the island but also supports the local economy and conservation efforts. While exploring these sites, tourists are encouraged to engage with local guides and use services that promote sustainable tourism, ensuring that Malta's heritage is preserved for future generations. Each site's specific location and offerings contribute to a memorable journey through Malta's vibrant history and dynamic cultural scene.

Useful Apps and Websites

In Malta, navigating through various activities and managing your time efficiently can be greatly aided by a selection of useful apps and websites designed to enhance the experience of both residents and visitors. Here's an overview of some highly recommended resources:

1. **Malta Public Transport App:** Vital for navigating the bus system, offering real-time updates, route planning, and stop information to seamlessly connect you to various attractions across the islands.

2. **Visit Malta App & Website:** Developed by the Malta Tourism Authority, these resources are central for tourists, providing a wealth of information on attractions, local events, and cultural festivals, complete with guides on how to get tickets and directions.

3. **Booking.com App:** A preferred tool for booking a variety of accommodations in Malta, featuring user reviews, detailed property descriptions, and the convenience of direct booking.

4. **WeatherBug or AccuWeather Apps:** Essential for real-time weather updates, helping you plan your day around Malta's climate, ensuring your activities match the weather conditions.

5. **XE Currency Converter & Revolut or Wise Apps:** These apps are indispensable for financial management, offering features like currency conversion, expense tracking, and budget management. They facilitate economic handling of expenditures during your stay.

6. **HSBC Malta App:** Useful for those requiring banking services, providing easy access to

account management, money transfers, and ATM locations throughout Malta.

7. **Malta Info Guide Website:** An extensive source for learning about Malta's offerings, from historical insights to dining options and nightlife, ensuring a well-rounded understanding of the island.

8. **First Aid Malta App:** Provides essential first aid information, a crucial tool for dealing with any unexpected medical issues, ensuring safety during your travels.

9. **Realtor Malta Website:** Offers comprehensive listings for those interested in renting or buying property, useful for longer stays or those considering relocating to Malta.

10. **Tallinja App:** Enhances the use of Malta's bus system by allowing users to manage their travel

card for bus rides, proving particularly helpful for frequent travelers.

11. **Official Malta Travel Guide:** The official website of the Malta Tourism Authority offers detailed planning resources, from festivals to essential tourist information, making it an invaluable tool for first-time and returning visitors alike.

12. **Google Maps App:** Indispensable for navigation and mapping in Malta, Google Maps provides detailed directions, whether you're driving, walking, or using public transit. It includes points of interest, tourist attractions, and local businesses, making it easy to find your way around the islands.

These tools collectively offer a robust support system for your travels in Malta, ensuring that you can navigate, plan, and enjoy your trip with ease.

CONCLUSION

This small island group, nestled in the Mediterranean Sea, offers a rich array of experiences that defy its modest size. From the historic lanes of Valletta and Mdina, adorned with baroque buildings, to the peaceful countryside of Gozo and the inviting blue waters surrounding the islands, Malta is a place where travelers can dive deep into a unique mix of cultures, histories, and natural splendors.

In this guide, we've covered everything you need to know to plan and enjoy a trip to Malta, providing thorough details on the major sites, from UNESCO World Heritage Sites to lesser-known spots worth visiting. We've also explored Maltese cuisine, reflecting the island's dynamic history and cultural exchanges. Moreover, we've offered practical tips on choosing places to stay, ways to travel around, and how to navigate the islands easily, ensuring every visitor finds something that suits their taste, whether it's luxury, adventure, or cultural immersion.

Personalizing your visit to Malta, whether it's through historical tours, culinary experiences, arts and culture, outdoor activities, or leisure and wellness, promises a uniquely fulfilling trip. Interacting with locals, participating in festivals and embracing traditions, and practicing sustainable tourism not only enhance your travel experience but also help preserve the cultural and natural treasures of Malta.

Malta presents a tapestry of experiences, each element a story, taste, or memory ready to be explored. This guide is your invitation to discover and cherish the enchantment of Malta. From strolling through ancient cities, swimming in stunning waters, to experiencing the hospitality of the Maltese people, your journey is set to be remarkable. As you explore each place and uncover each attraction, keep in mind that the real beauty of Malta lies not only in its landmarks but in the spirit of adventure, connection, and appreciation for this Mediterranean gem.

Printed in Great Britain
by Amazon